ADVICE FROM THE TOP

ADVICE FROM THE TOP

What Minority Women Say about Their Career Success

Valencia Campbell

PRAEGER

An Imprint of ABC-CLIO, LLC

A B C ⬤ C L I O

Santa Barbara, California • Denver, Colorado • Oxford, England

Library of Congress Cataloging-in-Publication Data

Advice from the top : what minority women say about their career success / by Valencia Campbell.
    p. cm.
   Includes bibliographical references and index.
   ISBN 978–0–313–35858–6 (hbk. : alk. paper) — ISBN 978–0–313–35859–3 (ebook)
1. Minority women executives. 2. Success in business. 3. Career development. 4. Women—
Vocational guidance. 5. Success. I. Title.
HD6054.3.C36   2009
658.4′09082—dc22   2009012193

13 12 11 10 9   1 2 3 4 5

This book is also available on the World Wide Web as an eBook.
Visit www.abc-clio.com for details.

ABC-CLIO, LLC
130 Cremona Drive, P.O. Box 1911
Santa Barbara, California 93116-1911

This book is printed on acid-free paper ∞

Manufactured in the United States of America

This book is dedicated to women everywhere who lend their support to others who are trying to achieve their career dreams and goals. It also dedicated to my parents, Mrs. Eula Preuitt and A. G. Preuitt (dec.), who instilled in me the desire to strive for success in all aspects of my life: family, employment, academic, and community service.

CONTENTS

PREFACE

Over the years, books and articles on workplace success have received a great deal of attention. Not surprisingly, much continues to be written about how women have fared in the workplace. However, this book aims to build on our knowledge of successful minority women, an area that has received far less attention. Although I believe we minority women have indeed made significant gains in the workplace since our days of being concentrated in service occupations, it is extremely important that minority women across a wide variety of occupational fields continue to share stories about their career success. By doing so, women will not have to repeat some of the same mistakes in seeking advancement opportunities. Further, we can gain a greater understanding of what it takes to succeed in certain fields that some women think are off limits to them.

This book seeks to increase our understanding of workplace issues that women sometimes face due to their gender or racial identity. Often women beginning their careers may start off well-equipped academically, full of energy and drive, only to confront a workplace whose culture does not value these commendable qualities in women or minorities. At other times, women may join a workplace that actually has policies in place, support networks, and managers who want to see them excel as the team works to accomplish the organization's mission. By sharing the workplace experiences of 14 extraordinary minority women, future generations can indeed profit from their reflections about their chosen occupational field. However, this book goes beyond a mere profile of the accomplishments of these 14 women. It also examines their views of success, describes the obstacles they encountered, and offers advice from each one. The women range from chief executive officers of their own companies to those who have held high-level government positions and those who have led large public school systems. You can see from their shared stories that these women have a great deal to say about what it took for them to succeed, sometimes against gender, race, or other workplace barriers.

The women selected for this book reveal certain truths that I hope each reader will take to heart—namely, that it is okay to have your own definition of career success. Through their comments and advice you can develop your own plan to find ways to move to the top levels of your chosen career, whether it is working in government, education, politics, or the legal field or working for yourself or some other choice. Their seminal advice will prove useful regardless of the choices you make.

This book contains six chapters: Chapter 1: Women's Definitions of Career Success, Chapter 2: Views on Career Success, Chapter 3: Successful Women Tell Their Stories, Chapter 4: Factors Responsible for Career Success, Chapter 5: Obstacles to Minority Women's Career Success and What to Do about Them, and Chapter 6: Looking Ahead: Some Career Fields That Need More Minority Women.

By reading these workplace experiences, I hope that more and more of you will share your own stories in order to leave a lasting legacy for our daughters, sisters, friends, and others who want to do their part to improve the status of women in our society.

ACKNOWLEDGMENTS

My deepest thanks goes to the 14 extraordinary women who shared their stories about their professional careers. These busy executives made special arrangements to find the time to answer my interview questions in their entirety. In some instances, the women were in the middle of handling multimillion-dollar business deals or just returning from important meetings abroad. Some had tremendous pressures on their time because they were highly sought after public figures. All of the women freely shared insights from their childhood, teen, and adult years regarding their quest to realize their career dreams. Note: *As this book was going to press, I was deeply saddened to learn of the news of Dr. Deagelia "Dely" Pena's passing. I know that she would have been so proud of the women who will have the opportunity to benefit from her words of wisdom and encouragement.*

9to5, National Association of Working Women provided the impetus and support needed for a project of this scope. For it was through my work with this organization, and the hundreds of women—and minority women, in particular —who called on us for help, that I realized that future generations of women would learn much if we could identify those factors that accomplished women believed were most responsible for their career success. Hopefully, they will avoid some of the pitfalls identified in this book, too.

The Richard R. Green Institute for Teaching and Learning provided support as well by conducting literature searches that were particularly germane to the focus of this project.

A special thanks to my editor, Jeff Olson of Greenwood Publishing Group, whose invaluable assistance made this book a reality. He believed in my book proposal and offered me a contract. His belief in the work that I wanted to share with young minority women allowed me to make what I hope will be a lasting contribution to the women who want to succeed in the workplace. Jeff's guidance and editorial assistance greatly improved this project. Many thanks to Hillary Claggett, Bridget Austiguy-Preschel, and Maureen Molloy as well.

My family deserves an ovation for their outstanding support. My sister, Sheila, and my brothers, Alvin, Gene, Martin, and Kenneth, wanted to know how the book was progressing and were anxious to learn when the book would be published. I owe a great debt of gratitude to them for all rising to the occasion when our family faced one of the most difficult challenges of our life—the sudden illness of our mom from a major stroke in January 2008. Their help in coordinating the family responsibilities regarding her treatment and daily affairs made it possible for me to keep writing even when I felt overwhelmed. Thankfully, mom never lost her speech or her reasoning and is making good progress toward a full recovery now. My faith in God sustained me during this difficult time. My husband, Paul, Sr., provided his unconditional support throughout this writing project, even when the demands of this book competed with our family plans. Also, I really appreciate the comments and questions he raised about some of the material that I chose to present. Hopefully, I have captured the comments of the women interviewed for this book in a way that is informative and interesting. My daughter, Annika, and son, Paul, Jr., were a constant source of encouragement along the way, too, with their many thoughtful questions about having a successful career

Finally, to my other family members and friends, too many to name here, I am grateful for your encouraging telephone calls and notes when I need them most.

Chapter 1

WOMEN'S DEFINITIONS OF CAREER SUCCESS

Much has been written in both the popular and professional literature about minority women who have achieved success in their careers.[1] Typically, these discussions profile the wealth of the women and explain whether they acquired a high social status through marriage or by holding a top position in government or in the private sector. Occasionally, their role in affecting change in American society is chronicled.[2] Further, women homemakers have been identified as successful based on their outstanding service to their local community.[3] Not surprisingly, out of these myriad profiles, you are likely to be intrigued by the many notions of success similar to the following:

- Sylvia Rimm, who achieved fame from having her research featured on Oprah Winfrey's show, *Oprah,* defines success as "personal fulfillment."[4] She does not define it as a significant title or sizable paycheck.
- According to another writer, Laura Davis, "Success is the ability to vision. It's about passion. It's a lifestyle. Men think success is a target you either hit or miss. Women get more joy out of life because they make success a process, not an end result."[5]
- Academic scholar Lia Wolf-Wende measures success based on high educational achievement (Ph.D.) or on being listed in various Marquis *Who's Who* reference books.[6]
- Cecilia Northcutt defined successful career women as those who have been recognized by their peers by virtue of having been either nominated for recognition or selected by a professional organization, civic group, women's recognition event, or employer.[7]

Accordingly, this book explores how a select group of minority women define success and seeks to identify the factors that they believe contributed to their career advancement. These women's stories are inspirational because each one of them grew up during a time of vastly changing social, economic, and political conditions in American society. Some of the women described here are similar to those studied a decade earlier in Dorothy Ehrhart-Morrison's book, *No Mountain High Enough.* They grew up in the 1940s and 1950s when, as Ehrhart-Morrison vividly points out, success in the minority community may have meant obtaining a college degree and earning a decent income.[8] During that time, many of the better-paying positions were closed to minorities. As Ehrhart-Morrrison notes, "It took the civil rights movement of the 1960s, the women's movement of the 1970s, affirmative action and other structural changes in society to provide more career opportunities to women."[9] The 14 women who were interviewed for this book have a great deal to say about what it took for them to rise to the top.

I wrote this book as a way to help young minority women realize their career goals. Often, minority women must overcome the double hurdle of race and gender barriers in American society. By sharing the views and advice of these women, it is my hope that young women today will obtain useful information they can use to build their own successful career.

You will learn how 14 extraordinary women define success, including the factors they consider responsible for their career success, the obstacles they encountered, and the advice they offer to young women today. Twelve of the women I interviewed were African Americans. One was Filipino and another was Hispanic. You will learn more about these women in Chapter 3, but for now the titles (at the time of the interview) and background of the women included in this book are as follows. Some have since moved on to other positions, and I have included updated information where available.

- **Debra Lee,** president and chief operating officer, Black Entertainment Television (BET)
- **Cathy Hughes,** founder and chairperson, Radio One, Inc.
- **Andrea Roane,** anchor, 9 Eyewitness News
- **Eunice Dudley,** chief financial officer, Dudley Products
- **Iris Metts,** superintendent of schools for Prince George's County, Maryland
- **Zina Pierre,** special assistant to the president for intergovernmental affairs in the White House
- **Jane Smith,** chief executive officer, Business & Professional Women USA (BPW)
- **Gwendolyn Calvert Baker,** director of social justice, American Educational Research Association
- **Rachel Petty,** vice president for academic affairs, University of the District of Columbia
- **Gail Nordmoe,** executive director, The Richard Green Institute
- **Deagelia Pena,** senior professional associate, Major Teacher's Union
- **Beatrice Muglia,** pathologist, Wheeling Hospital

- **Rondalyn Kane,** deputy director, Women's Bureau, U.S. Department of Labor
- **Jocelyn Bramble,** publisher, *Baltimore Times, Prince George's County Times,* and *Annapolis Times*

WHAT SUCCESS MEANS TO MINORITY WOMEN

As mentioned, success has a variety of meanings to women in both the popular and professional literature. These factors include personal fulfillment, the ability to maintain a clear vision, high academic achievement, and recognition by peers. Those definitions were not necessarily equated with the accumulation of great wealth. How do our women contributors compare with this literature? Does success mean something different for the minority women in this book? Let us see what success means to the 14 women profiled in this book.

SUCCESS IS ABOUT SETTING GOALS AND ACHIEVING THEM

The accumulation of wealth was not necessarily part of the definition of success mentioned by the women I interviewed. Although their definitions varied, the notion of setting a goal and achieving that goal was a consistent theme for 11 of the 14 women interviewed.

News anchor Andrea Roane, for example, said, "Success is accomplishing goals you set for yourself. It can include having a good marriage, healthy children and parents, and having faith to share what I have accomplished in my career. That means helping young artists or good students in their careers." Andrea's definition extends beyond her career. Although she emphasized accomplishing her goals, Roane's remarks indicate that the importance of her family life and sharing her knowledge with others, including aspiring youth, are key aspects of her definition of success.

Medical doctor Beatrice Muglia said, "Success is forming goals—big or small—that represent your own expectations and (then) achieving those goals. I don't define success in terms of money. It really is how happy you are with your life and what you are doing." A critical ingredient of Muglia's definition is the emphasis that you set your own expectations on what you want to accomplish rather than look to what others want you to achieve. Muglia's point cannot be overemphasized, since you probably can think of situations in which your parents, friends, aunts, uncles, and so forth may have asked if you're going to be a teacher, a doctor, a nurse, a business owner, like your mom or dad? Perhaps the questioner may have had a particular profession in mind based on their dreams for you, irrespective of what you had in mind. You should remember, however, that setting your own goals related to the type of career you want still leaves room to consider the recommendations offered by parents, relatives, or other individuals who are close to you or who have traveled the path before you. You can miss a lot of great opportunities by not considering the advice of others just because you want to do it your way and "make your own mistakes."

To amplify Muglia's point, let me give you a recent example of what I mean by a missed opportunity in the political arena. I received a notice from the White House that was widely distributed to community groups and other organizations throughout the country seeking young people who were interested in internship opportunities for the summer of 2008. I passed on this information to several young people and friends in the community, but none of the individuals that I spoke to were interested. Additionally, none of my friends heard from anyone on their distribution list asking about the position. You might surmise that perhaps they did not want to be involved in politics. That may be true enough. However, some of those who turned down this amazing opportunity may have had friends who would have been interested instead. Since I never heard from anyone, this seems to be a clear example of a missed opportunity. Those who were not interested in the position did not forward this information to others in their social or professional networks judging from the response that I received.

Radio magnate Cathy Hughes and educators Iris Metts, Rachel Petty, Gwendolyn Baker, Deagelia "Dely" Pena, and Gail Nordmoe were among the nine other women who viewed success in relationship to the goals that they set. Similarly, success involved setting goals, too, for newspaper owner Joy Bramble and former government manager Rondalyn Kane.

Cathy Hughes defined her success as "a work in progress," stating that "you reach certain milestones and set new ones." For Hughes, this definition seems to allow her to be forward looking. In one example from her radio business, which will be discussed in more detail in Chapter 3, Hughes said she faced a lot of rejection in seeking financing. Once financing was obtained, however, she quickly decided to purchase another radio station. Thus, Hughes began to set new goals after reaching that milestone. She rose to that challenge after suffering many setbacks.

Former school superintendent Iris Metts said simply, "Success means setting specific professional goals and achieving them." Metts explained that she knew that she wanted to work in the educational field. She did not set an immediate goal of becoming a superintendent, but as you will learn from her story, her initial career choice of becoming a teacher put her on the path to move up in the educational field.

University administrator Rachel Petty said, "Success is realized when a person actualizes his or her goals. Since goals shift, it is a process of pursuit. You obtain one goal, you move forward with others. If you are truly committed, money will come." Petty's view, like that of radio magnate Cathy Hughes, has the element of constant pursuit in meeting a goal and, once achieved, setting new goals. Petty added the idea that money will come based on your commitment to achieving your goals. This optimism about money is not surprising given that Petty was trained as a psychologist. Psychologists tend to view the importance of various individual traits, such as commitment and drive, as key in explaining successful careers. These personal qualities are discussed in more detail in Chapter 2, Views of Career Success.

Assistant superintendent Gail Nordmoe, educator Dely Pena, and newspaper publisher Jocelyn Bramble specifically de-emphasized the idea of equating money with success in their comments.

Gail Nordmoe said, "It is the way in which an individual believes their personal and professional goals have been met. It is possible to not make money and have a sense of success."

Deagelia Pena indicated, "Success is achieving something you want to achieve in your life. I don't believe it is defined by money, although you do need a basic amount of funds, much like an artist who wants to keep her artwork on display."

Jocelyn Bramble said, "Success means achieving your goal, feeling satisfied and happy where you are. It is personal. I never thought about it in terms of money."

IT IS ABOUT HELPING OTHERS

Although Gwendolyn Baker emphasized the notion of achieving your goal, she added another dimension not mentioned by the other women. She said, "[Success] is twofold, accomplishing my goals that I have set, which includes contributing to improving the lives of other people. It means feeling good about what you have accomplished and has nothing to do with money."

Zina Pierre was studying the ministry at the time of my interview with her. Although she held a top job as a political appointee in the Clinton White House, her definition of success revolved around the notion of helping others, too. "Success is based on how well you take what you have been blessed with to help someone else," Pierre said. She mentioned that she was currently acting as a mentor to several students regarding their career goals.

IT IS ABOUT YOUR VALUES

Rondalyn Kane told me that when she was younger, she felt that success meant obtaining certain goals in her career and making money. "Since I have accomplished the goals that I set for myself, now I am interested in doing what fulfills me spiritually; that is, doing a job that fulfills a greater human good and making a contribution to society. I want to fulfill God's expectation."

Jane Smith said three important values define her career achievements. First, having solid personal and professional relationships is an important value. Next, religious and spiritual values aided her career success. Her third value had to do with the accumulation of wealth "for my descendants."

IT IS ABOUT MONEY TOO

What happened to the idea that fame and fortune constitute success, as is often popularized in the media? Aside from the idea of accumulating wealth mentioned by Jane Smith, two business executives, Eunice Dudley and Debra Lee, framed their idea of obtaining wealth in their definitions of success.

Eunice Dudley, the chief financial officer of Dudley Products, a multimillion-dollar hair products company, said, "Success is being healthy, gaining some wealth, and being wise with it. You should remain humble if you obtain anything." Dudley's caution about being wise with the money that you acquire is probably one of her guiding principles in her role as the chief financial officer of her family business. At that level, she is able to see all of the sources of income generated by the business, including where the money is spent, and make decisions that will keep the business on sound financial ground. Aside from obtaining wealth, the fact that health was a salient dimension of Dudley's definition of success should be underscored as well. In my opinion, what good is it to obtain thousands of dollars or even millions without being healthy enough to enjoy it all? Women, in particular, must guard their workplace activities in order that potential stressors sometimes associated with their gender do not overwhelm them. The gender issue is discussed in a later chapter regarding obstacles that impede minority women's career success.

Debra Lee, the former president and chief operating officer of BET Holdings, placed her definition of success in financial terms related to how well her business is doing. Specifically, she connects her success to the business goals of the television industry. "Success to me means ratings on programming, our profitability," Lee said. "We create wealth for our shareholders." In other words, keeping her cable television audience watching BET programming was foremost on the mind of this multimillionaire executive. Lee, as you will learn later, received a great deal of the credit for the tremendous role she played in helping BET Founder Robert Johnson and his former wife, Sheila, build their cable television empire. Robert Johnson later sold the company to Viacom for $3 billion.

An appraisal of these women's views shows a common theme—setting a goal and achieving that goal. Nearly all of the women did not equate money with success despite the fact that all of them have achieved salaries well above the average salary of women wage earners today. Another interesting aspect of many of the women studied include notions of feeling a sense of fulfillment in their relationships with family and friends and of making a contribution through helping others.

If you are one of those persons who equates money with success in addition to some of the factors mentioned previously, then following are a few facts about some of the highest-paying occupations regardless of one's racial status.

HIGHEST-PAYING OCCUPATIONS

In Census 2000, 20 occupations were identified as having the highest median earnings for men and women.[10] That means that 50 percent or more of those that the Census Bureau interviewed made above or below the salary

Table 1.1
Top 10 Highest Paid Occupations Reported by the U. S. Bureau of the Census

Women	Men
Physicians and surgeons	Physicians and surgeons
Engineering managers	Dentists
Dentists	Chief executives
Lawyers	Lawyers
Optometrists	Judges, magistrates, and other judicial workers
Pharmacists	Natural science managers
Chief executives	Optometrists
Economists	Actuaries
Computer/information system managers	Engineering managers
Sales engineers	Economists

listed in the report. Physicians and surgeons was the highest-paid occupation for both men and women. The median salary for men was $140,000, while that for women was only $88,000. Indeed, the median salaries for men exceeded that of women in most occupations. Although the complete listing is available in the Census Bureau's 2004 report, the 10 occupations listed in Table 1.1 provide an idea of how men and women fared.[11] Data were not available by minority status.

After the 2010 census, you will be able to determine the most recent data on the highest-paid occupations. That information will be quite useful for those of you who are considering some of these occupations. The last chapter in this book will provide an examination of the current status of minority women in selected fields, such as business, education, law, politics, government, and medicine. This information should help you understand other issues you are likely to confront as you strive to achieve success in your chosen field.

NOTES

1. Laura Randolph, "Superwoman: How They Manage to Almost Do It All," *Ebony* 43 no. 6 (1998); Caroline Clarke, "Take A Lesson: Today's Achievers on How They Made It and What They Learned Along the Way," and Sara Cook, "Cultivate the Habits of Highly Successful Women," *Women in Higher Education,* 7 no.11 (1998); Patricia Reid-Merritt, *Sister Power: How Phenomenal Black Women Are Rising to the Top* (New York: John Wiley & Sons, Inc., 1996).

2. Amy Alexander, *Fifty Black Women Who Changed America* (New Jersey: Birch Lane, 1999); Gene Landrum, *Profiles of Female Genius: Thirteen Creative Women Who Changed the World* (New York: Prometheus Books, 1996).

3. Sylvia Rimm, *How Jane Won: 55 Successful Women Show How They Grew From Ordinary Girls to Extraordinary Women* (New York: Crown Business, 2000).

4. Ibid.

5. Sara Cook, "Cultivate the Habits of Highly Successful Women," *Women in Higher Education,* 7 no. 11 (1998).

6. Lia Wolf-Wendel, "Models of Excellence," *The Journal of Higher Education* 69 no.2 (2000): 141–186.

7. Cecelia Northcutt, *Successful Career Women* (New York: Greenwood Publishing Group, 1991).

8. Dorothy Ehrhart-Morrison, *No Mountain High Enough: Secrets of Successful African American Women* (Berkeley, California: Conari Press, 1997).

9. Ibid.

10. Daniel Weinberg, "Some Evidence from Census 2000 About Earnings by Detailed Occupation for Men and Women," *Census 2000 Special Reports* (Washington, D.C.: U. S. Department of Commerce, Economic and Statistics Administration, 2004).

11. See the appendix of the U.S. Department of Labor's *Occupational Outlook Handbook 2008–2009* for descriptions of some of these positions. More information on projected employment figures is found there also.

Chapter 2

VIEWS ON CAREER SUCCESS

Y ou are likely to be familiar with many of the popular views regarding the road to career success. These views are often given a great deal of media attention, but they usually reflect exceptional cases and rarely provide a reliable guide for advancement in the workplace. Despite their lack of reliability, these views have persisted. More than 30 years ago, Margaret Higginson and Thomas Quick's work, *The Ambitious Women's Guide to a Successful Career,* provided examples of popular-but-erroneous views that nonetheless have endured over time.[1]

POPULAR VIEW ON CAREER SUCCESS

The Higginson and Quick *Guide* included five approaches for explaining career success. They were the Cinderella theory, the Cream theory, the Puritan Ethic theory, the Jungle theory, and the Starlet theory. Let's take a quick glance at each of these conventional views before examining the theories that scholars and researchers have proposed in explaining career advancement.

Cinderella Theory

The Cinderella theory suggests that a woman can get ahead through an attention-getting stand-in performance for her boss. For example, her boss may be asked to give a major presentation to the organization's executive committee. Due to a conflict in his or her schedule, the woman may be asked to give the presentation instead. The woman does a great job in giving the presentation, attracting attention from higher-level executives who want to know more about her. As a result, she will then be promoted to a higher- level position.

According to Higginson and Quick, there are many problems with this viewpoint. The executive committee expects that it will receive a good presentation regardless of who gives it. The senior executives will probably give the credit for the presentation to the boss rather than to the stand-in person. Additionally, the substitute person would need more than one appearance before that committee to be seen as a "star."

Cream Theory

Those taking the Cream theory viewpoint believe that the best (most talented, brightest, etc.) people will automatically rise to the top. However, it is well known that executives at the top are not necessarily the most talented. Examinations of business organizations today show a range of factors that propelled these executives to the upper echelons of their professions.[2] They include networking and developing negotiating skills.

Still other studies on minority women show that many successful women do not move up sequentially.[3] Many women make a great deal of lateral movements as well. In other words, the women may have to transfer to other departments without getting a raise, and then they have to figure out the next steps to take in order to get ahead in their new environments. This course may take a great deal of planning to further determine their future direction.

Clearly, cream doesn't always rise to the top. Usually the ambitious person has to create a strategy, and pursue it vigorously, to achieve a desired position.

Puritan Ethic Theory

If you work hard and don't make waves, you are likely to be rewarded—at least according to the Puritan Ethic viewpoint. Again, according to Higginson and Quick, many hard workers don't rise very far in the organization because they are known for their reliability and thus are labeled as good and desirable subordinates. Unfortunately, for these diligent workers, managers often want them to stay where they are.

Jungle Theory

The survival of the fittest is the major premise of the Jungle theory point of view. The strongest, the most competitive, and the most political will get ahead. Here, Higginson and Quick note that it is not debatable that those who want to get ahead should be aware of the organization's climate and know what kind of behavior and attributes are most favored by those in power. In most cases, they note, coworkers, peers, and superiors will find ways of keeping those who trample on others from reaching their goal due to their feeling that the hard driver is a threat to the position that they hold.

Starlet Theory

The Starlet theory says that a woman's sexual appeal—and use of it—will help her progress in her career. Although some women may have gotten to the top this way, establishing a career involves many uncertainties and can become even more complicated when sex enters the picture. Sometimes women (and men) enter into consensual relationships without experiencing any negative effects to their job. However, major problems arise when women feel coerced into entering a sexual relationship in order to keep or to advance in their jobs. Also, women may refuse the advances of their supervisor and not receive promotions or other career-building assignments as a result. In the latter two instances, the requests for sexual favors could be considered a condition of the women keeping their jobs, which constitutes sexual harassment and complicates any woman's employment atmosphere in a negative way.

Clearly, the large number of sexual harassment cases reveal this complication when those involved in liaisons are subjected to questions about whether the liaisons were consensual or coerced and what effect, if any, the relationship had on the woman's employment status. The latest data filed with the Equal Employment Opportunity Commission (EEOC) and the state and local Fair Employment Practices Offices showed that 12,510 charges were filed in FY 2007, up from 12,056 in FY 2006. An examination of the facts of these and other cases would reveal that many were never consensual. Using sexual favors to advance in the workplace is never wise. You can sometimes avoid the nightmare of filing a sexual harassment complaint by making good decisions about romantic relationships.

SCIENTIFIC APPROACHES EXPLAINING SUCCESS

Now that we have debunked the popular viewpoints on how women can succeed in the workplace, let us turn to the professional literature to uncover more reliable explanations for career success. You should know, however, that social scientists, too, offer many competing views on how women achieve career success in their chosen fields. Often the concepts studied and methodologies employed (questionnaires, surveys, interviews) differ, which sometimes affect how candid the women are in sharing their career experiences. For example, I found that all of the women that I interviewed were quite responsive to the questions that I asked them. Nevertheless, I may have obtained even more information if they had received a mailed questionnaire and actually returned it to me, as this method may have given them more time to provide responses. The downside to the mail approach, of course, is that the recipient might not get it back in time for it to be useful or it may not be returned at all.

HOW PSYCHOLOGISTS EXPLAIN CAREER SUCCESS

Psychological approaches to explaining career success typically see personality as fundamental. Gene Landrum's study of 13 successful women summarizes several leading theorists whose views can be used to explain career success.[4] Carl Jung, for example, proposed a theory of archetypes believed to be products of a personal and collective unconscious. Jung's notion of psychological types was refined further by Myers and Briggs and David Kiersey. In essence, people exhibiting certain personality types defined by Jung and Myers and Briggs, such as extrovert/introvert, intuitive/thinking, or "visionary" (labeled Promethesus in Kiersey's theory), are expected to be more successful than others in certain careers. Landrum gives an example in which he posits that the rational-thinker type would make a terrible nurse and that accountants should be tested to make sure they are sensing-judging types in order to succeed in that career. Next, Landrum notes that Forkley devised a theory of testosterone behavior as a key factor in creativity, risk-taking, and competitiveness. Presumably, this helps explain men's dominance of high-level positions in the workforce. Finally, Landrum discusses the McClellan theory of motivation, or "needs theory," where achievement, power, and affiliation are the key factors driving people to excel.

Landrum points out that the research using the above approaches identifies 10 key success traits: charisma, competition, confidence, energy, independence, passion, perfection, temerity, tenacity, and intuitive vision. Landrum believes these factors were the foundation on which the 13 women he studied built their great success. Landrum's later study using secondary sources identified these same traits to explain the extraordinary success of 13 well-known black American women and men. Oprah Winfrey, Maya Angelou, and Shirley Chisholm were the three women in his study. Bill Cosby, Berry Gordy, Michael Jordan, Colin Powell, and Reginald Lewis were among the 10 men he studied.

HOW SOCIAL SCIENTISTS EXPLAIN CAREER SUCCESS

Social views that are used to explain career success generally focus on certain structural properties of group relations. External factors, rather than individual traits, are viewed as the most salient factors that promote or inhibit a woman's career success. Taking such a focus moves attention away from a blame-the-victim approach for not achieving career success. Although the role of intelligence, motivation, discipline, and a host of other psychological variables are recognized, factors external to the individual also affect their ability to achieve career success.

Ella Bell and Stella Nkomo's landmark eight-year study is indicative of research that use a social view in explaining the factors that shape the career experiences of black and white women.[5] In their framework, gender, race, and class are key interlocking elements. Specifically, they show how each of these concepts have been known to generate various expectations and beliefs that can promote or inhibit a woman's ability to reach her greatest potential, whether socially, politically, or economically.

According to these authors, gender, for example, does not represent just a classification to distinguish males from females. It is much more. "It is also a set of assumptions and beliefs on both individual and societal levels that affects the thoughts, feelings, behaviors, resources, and treatment of women and men."[6] They further note that in Western society, infants are taught to incorporate social orientations about appropriate roles for men and women and the relationships that exist between them. Within this context, one's gender can be seen as the primary vehicle that explains what happens to women in society. Indeed, the author notes, "throughout history and in every society, gender has been one of the major structures of domination perpetuated by "patriarchy."

Similarly, race is seen as more than a concept that classifies groups of people based on physical traits such as skin color. It denotes the meanings given to or attached to "phenotypical" differences among people. Bell and Nkomo argue that race has been used to maintain power in certain groups while weakening other groups.[7] Moreover, they add, prior to and even into the twentieth century, race determined a woman's political rights and social status. Nkomo and Bell maintain that "race still determines a woman's position within the labor market and her economic well-being."[8] In their view, race keeps minority women from completely participating in organizational life. In their previous work on the barriers to workplace advancement experienced by African Americans, they found that minority women managers reported facing greater scrutiny and extra challenges because of their race.

Another element of Bell and Nkomo's theoretical framework is social class, in which they use Gerda Lerner's definition of the concept. Social class is viewed as the degree of access one has to resources and to power.[9] According to the researchers, "a woman's social class determines her access to a variety of benefits such as economic power, political power, education and entry into important social networks."

Culture and history are two other elements important in guiding Bell and Nkomo's research, as they view the three key elements of race, gender, and class as being broadly affected by both culture and history. For them, culture shapes a woman's values and her career choices. Generally seen as comprising all aspects of the way of life associated with a group of people, culture includes language, beliefs, norms, values, customs, technology, and other components, according to sociologist Joseph Healy.[10] Bell and Nkomo argue that culture influences the "values a woman holds, the career choices she makes, and how she navigates the corporate arena."[11]

Bell and Nkomo's last element, history, is important in providing a context for understanding the career and lives of women who rose to a managerial level. The authors discuss how social norms and societal beliefs, among other things, usually reflect certain historical periods. In their view, this element is so critical in either opening new growth opportunities for women or in erecting roadblocks to opportunities. For example, think of how the civil rights movement, the black power movement, or the women's movement helped launch the careers of so many ordinary and famous Americans like Dorothy Height, C. DeLores Tucker, Shirley Chisholm, and Mae Jemison.

HUMAN CAPITAL THEORY

Another view that uses both social and individual traits as an explanation for success is the human capital theory, which sees the level of success achieved by an individual in society as a result of such assets as educational level, personal values, skills, and effort.[12] Education is seen as an investment in human capital. According to this theory, one would expect that the greater the investment in a person's human capital, the higher the probability of success.

Families, too, are seen as a key investment in human capital. Families help individuals through formal education and through socializing the individual in what is expected of them in a given situation. The role of the family is important in determining the likelihood of wealth or poverty over time.

SOCIAL CAPITAL THEORY

Another view that complements the human capital theory is known as the social capital theory. Although scholars have variously defined the concept, John Fields succinctly points out that an essential element of social capital theory is one's social network.[13] Social networks—think of the proverbial "old boys' network"— can be extremely important in bringing benefits to people. Indeed, one's relationships and how close one is to individual network members that have access to other resources can help substantially in pointing individuals to job leads, promotions, or other influential contacts. Being involved in a social network can create relationships of trust and tolerance.

According to David Halpern's 2005 work, *Social Capital,* the three components of social capital consist of networks (the interconnecting relationships between people), norms (the rules, values and expectations that govern social interaction), and sanctions (the punishment and rewards that enforce the norms). These three components influence each other.

Other scholars caution that social network groups and organizations have the means and sometimes the motive to exclude and subordinate others.[14] This means that one should be mindful that social networks could have negative implications as well. Additionally, these scholars contend that the very features of some organizations may hurt or help one's career.

ORGANIZATIONAL STRUCTURE THEORY

A central idea of this theory, according to scholars Carla Wiggins and Sarah Bowman, is that barriers are built into organizations that work either for or against career success. "Organizational structures, systems, processes and policies can directly or indirectly help or hamper one's career," they stated. Further, they acknowledge that many of the more explicit barriers, such as discrimination and unfair hiring practices, are against the law. However, certain features of the organization could still allow a glass ceiling to exist for women and minorities that would prevent them from reaching the top positions in their organizations. With that in mind, remember that there are still those in organizations who may discriminate against women and minorities in hiring practices and promotions even if it is against the law. In 1996, a case involving Texaco dominated the national broadcast and print media for months. In that case, Texaco executives were caught on tape using racial slurs against blacks and planning to destroy documents necessary to a lawsuit filed on behalf of the company's minority employees. A former white executive turned over the damaging evidence to the plaintiff's lawyers. When the tape was played in news offices across the country, Texaco decided to settle the lawsuit for $176 million. In this instance, people in the organization knew of discriminatory treatment of its minority employees but did not expect to get caught.

Now that you have a brief idea of some of the theories that can be used to explain career advancement in the workplace, our next focus will be to examine specific career fields more closely. The following sections describe the scholarly literature regarding women and advancement in education, the federal government, various other professions, and the business community. Bear in mind that the studies here represent a mere sample of the existing literature on this topic. For a more detailed discussion, see the original sources listed in the notes and bibliography.

STUDIES ON WOMEN ADVANCING IN EDUCATION

Lorenzo Jasso studied how minority women became school principals.[15] In his dissertation on the topic, he sought to determine the key factors related to obtaining this position and found noticeable differences between men and women regarding what they believed it took to attain a principal position in a K–12 school setting. Women rated such items as ambition, personality, verbal ability, education, and self-confidence higher than men did. Men, on the other hand, rated items like holding membership in professional organizations, physical appearance, being involved in work-related social activities, and having influential male sponsors higher than women did.

Another study by Suzanne De LaVergne examined factors associated with upward mobility in public school administration.[16] She found no significant difference between age, education, ethnicity, and marital status in the acquisition of administrative positions in public schools. In her study, successful administrators reported that being active in professional organizations was very beneficial. (You might recall that this is a key concept in the social capital literature.) The very successful administrators did not have mentors more frequently than did the less successfully ranked subjects. However, the more successful administrators did serve as mentors more often. Having a role model did not make a significant difference in the administrators' self-rating of success, but De La Vergne found that minority subjects indicated that it was important for the role model to be of the same gender and ethnicity.

Finally, Ponchitta Roberson conducted a study of the career path of women in higher education.[17] Her major focus was to describe how women access the ranks of senior-level administration in higher education at both public and private liberal arts institutions. The study sought to identify whether routes of entry differ for women administrators belonging to various ethnic groups. Another goal of the study was to provide women, especially minority women, who want to achieve senior administrative positions with the appropriate information for entry.

Although women administrators may occasionally come from outside the academic ranks, such as from a high-level corporate position, Roberson's findings showed that women administrators were generally selected from within the higher education community.[18] Typically, women met the traditional criteria of having advanced to their position from a lower-ranking academic position. For minority women seeking the dean position, the entry position for them was an associate, assistant, or chair position. All women who aspired to senior administrative positions saw obtaining a doctorate in education— Ed.D or Ph.D—as a necessity. Minority women felt that they worked twice as hard as their other female and male colleagues, and all women regardless of race felt that they worked much harder than their male colleagues. Her study shows the importance of two key elements of the human capital theory, education and individual efforts like working hard. Also, as Bell and Nkomo emphasized in their theoretical approach, the element of race figures prominently in this study of women in higher education. Other key findings revealed that these women increased their chances of promotion by volunteering at and/or attending conferences emphasizing diversity in the workplace.

Others have explored the extent to which attendance at a particular type of college or university has accounted for a women's career success.[19] After collecting data on the educational backgrounds of 126 successful women, Ledman, Miller, and Brown found that for white women, graduates of women's colleges were more likely to obtain career success than graduates of coeducational institutions. Obtaining a graduate degree influenced women's chances of success as well.

Researcher Betty Harper reviewed a great deal of the literature on whether attendance at a women's college versus a coeducational college made a difference in one's occupational status or earnings.[20] She believes socioeconomic status, ability, and characteristics of the school such as selectivity were actually responsible for the positive relationship between one's college choice and occupational status and earnings. In other words, attending a women's college does not necessarily translate into a higher job level or earnings than one's counterparts who attended coeducational institutions.

Studies on Women Advancing in the Federal Government

Studies exploring women's advancement opportunities in the federal government show once again the importance of various social factors. For example, Katherine Naff studied determinants of job advancement in the federal government and found gender to be an important factor in explaining career advancement.[21] Women who worked in the federal bureaucracy for less than 10 years and from 20 to 30 years did not advance in their professions as successfully as men did. The gender aspect persisted even when controlling for differences between the sexes in human capital factors, work habits, work opportunities, and personal circumstances.

The President's Interagency Council on Women report captured trend data for the percentage of women at the highest career levels and for those working in the Senior Executive Service (SES) of the federal government.[22] These data showed that the percentage of women in these high-level positions has increased some over the years. For example, the percentage of women in the SES was 5 percent in 1979, 10 percent in 1989, 19 percent in 1995, and 20 percent in 1996. Unfortunately, the President's Council did not report the figures for minority women. Given this small representation of women in general, however, it is quite likely that the figures for minority women alone would be much lower than those reported here.

More recent information complied by the General Accounting Office does give us a glimpse of how well minority women and African-American women, in particular, fared in their representation in these top SES jobs in the federal government. Overall, women as a group continued to make gains. For example, women held about one-fourth (25 percent) of the SES positions in 2000 and almost one-third (31 percent) in 2006.[23] As expected, these data show that the representation of African-American women in the top SES jobs is quite bleak, as only 4 percent of African-American women filled the SES ranks in both 2000 and 2006. American Indian/Alaska Native and Hispanic women held less than 1 percent of the SES jobs for both 2000 and 2006. Asian women moved from no representation in 2000 to almost 2 percent in 2006. Among women, then, white women held the highest proportion of the top SES positions, accounting for 19 percent in 2000 and 23 percent in 2006.

Additional findings from the President's Interagency Council on Women report (which are consistent with the past literature) show that women who chose to have children during their careers were especially disadvantaged in their advancement opportunities.

Studies of Minority Women Advancing in Various Professions in the Private Sector

Researchers Aguilar and Williams studied Hispanic and African-American women to find out the factors they believed most contributed to their career success.[24] They found that psychological factors (i.e., life satisfaction, personal strength such as persistence, determination, strong self esteem and self motivation) and some social factors, such as ethnic pride, religious values, and family support, determined these women's success. Although the researchers use the term personal strength, it is clear from their examples that the term could be used interchangeably with the psychological traits model discussed earlier.

Other interesting similarities and differences emerged between African-American and Hispanic women. African-American women most frequently mentioned education as a contributing factor in their career success, followed by a variety of indicators of personal strength. Like their African-American counterparts, Hispanic women most frequently mentioned education too, a key element of the human capital theoretical model mentioned previously. However, job satisfaction was the next most frequently mentioned factor by Hispanic women rather than personal strength indicators. A surprising outcome of this study was the finding that both poverty and discrimination were seen as strengths because those experiences made some of the women more determined to succeed.

According to Aguilar and Williams, the women they studied typically set clear goals for themselves and were realistic about the opportunities they were afforded and the barriers to achievement they experienced. The women identified themselves as being in professions of social work, nursing, medicine, administration, political science, psychology, education, and communication.[25]

STUDIES ON WOMEN ADVANCING IN THE BUSINESS COMMUNITY

Studies from the business community typically focus on profiles of women entrepreneurs who started their own successful businesses or became managers in profitable companies.[26] A few minority women are sometimes included, but rarely do the authors provide a theoretical lens to assist the reader in uncovering key factors thought to be important in explaining their career success. Readers are often left to assemble their own notions about how the women achieved their success.

A 1998 study by Friedman, Kane, and Cornfield, however, is illustrative of research that uses a social framework to explain career success.[27] In that study, the authors examined the effectiveness of network groups among black managers. The authors note that female and minority network groups are not understood very well, and no quantitative analysis had taken place on their impact on minority employees. Remember, the major premise of the social network theory or social capital theory is that network groups should enhance the social resources available to women and minorities and thus enhance their chances of career success. These researchers found that network groups had a positive overall impact on the career optimism of black managers, and that this occurs primarily via enhanced mentoring. They found that the network groups did not produce greater discrimination. A negative aspect of the network group occurred for a few managers where they experienced increased social isolation.

The Bell and Nkomo study mentioned earlier in the chapter compared and contrasted the careers and life experiences of black and white women managers.[28] Their work highlighted the life and career struggles of successful black and white women in corporate America. Using a social framework, they found that the combined effects of race and gender created very different organizational identities and career experiences for the women. They found, not surprisingly, that black and white women traveled very separate paths to the doors of corporate America, a finding that highlights the need for continued study of these two groups as separate entities.

Indeed, the influence of race and gender emerged as salient factors in both the life history interviews Bell and Nkomo conducted as well as in the results of their random survey of 1,461 African-American and white women managers. For example, they found that minority women faced an even greater hurdle than the glass ceiling—a concrete wall. The glass ceiling represents the inability of women to rise above a certain level in the corporate hierarchy, but the concrete wall is more persistent. In their view, the concrete wall manifested itself in six ways: daily doses of racism, being held to a higher standard, the invisibility vise, exclusion from informal networks, challenges to authority, and hollow company commitment to the advancement of minorities.[29] Similarly, their national survey showed that black women managers (39 percent) were more likely to believe that they were behind in career progress than white women managers (25 percent).[30] In addition, they found that African-American women managers were more inclined to feel that they had to outperform their white colleagues—both male and female—in order to succeed. African-American women viewed their relationships with their bosses and colleagues less favorably. As a result, African-American women reported receiving less collegial support than did the white women managers in the survey. On the other hand, white women managers were more positive about their organizations' overall management of race and gender relations and commitment to the advancement of women and people of color.

What Does It All Mean?

Not surprisingly, a review of this literature has shown considerable variation in factors associated with achieving career success. In some of the studies just reviewed, certain human capital and social capital factors (i.e., education, race, gender, networking and volunteering, or attending a special focus college or university) have emerged as being important, while in other studies these same factors were seen to be less important. For example, in the Roberson study, a doctoral degree was a necessity in achieving a senior-level academic position in a university. Regardless of which approach you believe is most useful, it is often helpful to identify at least one approach that you can apply to help you understand the career advancement of successful women.

In the chapters to follow, you will learn which, if any, of the factors uncovered in this literature review were mentioned by the minority women I interviewed. By focusing exclusively on minority women, this book will help fill an important gap in the literature on the factors that contribute to the career success of minority women.

Notes

1. Margaret Higginson and Thomas Quick, *The Ambitious Women's Guide to a Successful Career* (New York: Amacom, 1975).

2. Ellie Wylie, *Conversations With Uncommon Women* (New York: American Management Association, 1996).

3. A. B. Revere, "Black Women Superintendents in the United States 1984–85," *Journal of Negro Education* 56 (1987): 510–520; Ella Bell and Stella Nkomo, *Our Separate Ways* (Massachusetts: Harvard Business School Press, 2001); and various chapters (especially Ancella Livers "Black Women in Management," Margaret Foegen Karsten ed., *Gender, Race and Ethnicity in the Workplace: Issues and Challenges for Today's Organizations* (Connecticut: Praeger, 2006).

4. Gene Landrum, *Profiles of Female Genius: Thirteen Creative Women Who Changed the World* (New York: Promethus, 1996); and Gene Landrum, *Profiles of Black Success* (New York: Promethus, 1999).

5. Bell and Nkomo, *Our Separate Ways,* 16–17.

6. Ibid., 16.

7. Ibid., 17.

8. Ibid.

9. Gerda Lerner, *Why History Matters* (New York: Oxford University Press, 1999), 181.

10. See Joseph Healey, *Race, Ethnicity, Gender and Glass* (California Pine Forge Press, 1995), 539, for a more detailed discussion of culture.

11. Bell and Nkomo, *Our Separate Ways,* 18.

12. See discussions by the following authors describing this theory: Craig Calhoun and others, eds., *Dictionary of the Social Sciences* (London: Oxford University Press, 2002), 216; and Carla Wiggins and Sarah Bowman, "Career Success and Life Satisfaction for Female and Male Health Care Managers," *Hospital Topics* 78 (2000): 5.

13. John Field, *Social Capital* (London: Routledge, 2003).

14. M. K. Smith, "Social Capital." *The Encyclopedia of Informal Education,* ed., 2007 www.infed.org/biblio/social_capital.htm (accessed May 27, 2008); and Wiggins and Bowman, "Career Success and Life Satisfaction for Female and Male Health Care Managers."

15. Lorenzo Jasso, "Variables Related to Minority Attainment of the Principalship" (Ph.D. dissertation, Drake University, 1991).

16. Suzanne De La Vergne, "Factors Affecting Upward Mobility of Minority Women in School Administration" (Ph.D. dissertation, U.S. International University, 1991). The De La Vergne study respondents included administrators such as superintendents, directors, principals, and assistant principals. She mailed questionnaires to 438 school

administrators. She obtained a response rate of 44.7 percent, with 191 useable questionnaires.

17. Ponchitta Roberson, "Career Paths and Profiles of Women as Senior Administrators in Higher Education" (Ph.D. dissertation, George Washington University, 1998).

18. In Roberson's study, 268 women were chosen through a stratified random sample selection process to complete a questionnaire. The response rate was 60 percent, which is considered to be a good representation of the population studied.

19. R. E. Ledman, M. Miller, and D. R. Brown, "Successful Women and Women's Colleges: Is There an Intervening Variable in the Reported Relationship?" *Sex Roles* 33 (1995): 489–497; and L. E. Wolf-Wendel, "Models of Excellence: The Baccalaureate Origins of Successful European American Women, African American Women and Latinos," *Journal of Higher Education* 69 (1998): 141–186.

20. Betty Harper, "Women's College in an Era of Gender Equity: A Review of the Literature on the Effects of Institutional Gender on Women," *Higher Education Review* 3 (2006): 1–23.

21. Katherine Naff, "The Glass Ceiling Revisited: Determinants of Federal Job Advancement.," *Policy Studies Review* 13 (1995): 249–72.

22. Presidents Interagency Council on Women: America's Commitment to Women (Washington, D.C.: Government Printing Office, 2000).

23. General Accounting Office, Human Capital Diversity in the Federal SES and Senior Levels of the U.S. Postal Service (Washington, D.C.) GAO-07838T.

24. M. Aguilar and Lorece Williams, "Factors Contributing to the Success and Achievement of Minority Women," *Affilia* 8 (1991): 410–423.

25. The Aguilar and Williams study involved a non-systematic selected sample of 164 Hispanic women and 160 African-American women, so the study findings cannot be considered representative of a larger population of the two groups.

26. A. Mikaelian, *Women Who Mean Business: Success Stories of Women Over Forty* (New York: William Morrow and Company, 1999); Augusto Failde and William Doyle, *Latino Success: Insights from 100 of America's Most Powerful Latino Business Professionals* (New York: Simon and Schuster, 1996); and Nikki Mitchell, *The New Color of Success: Twenty Young Black Millionaires Tell You How They're Making It* (California: Prima, 1999).

27. R. Friedman, M. Kane and D. B. Cornfield, "Social Support and Career Optimism: Examining the Effectiveness of Network Groups Among Black Managers," *Human Relations* 51 (1998): 1155–1177.

28. Bell and Nkomo, *Our Separate Ways.*

29. Ibid., 140.

30. The Bell and Nkomo study had a sample of 120 women (80 black and 40 white) for their life history interviews and 825 respondents, with a 56 percent response rate from their random survey. They oversampled black women in their interviews since research on the effects of gender, race, and class on the career paths of women has been under investigated.

Chapter 3

SUCCESSFUL WOMEN TELL THEIR STORIES

The 14 minority women that you are about to meet offer inspiration for anyone who wants to learn from their career experiences. Some are well-known multimillionaire business owners like Cathy Hughes and Eunice Dudley. Others—such as Jane Smith—held top jobs leading national nonprofit organizations as president and CEO. One, Zina Pierre, was among the few black women who landed a key position working in the executive branch of government—the White House. Debra Lee made millions after working in the number-two position for years at the Black Entertainment Network (BET) when it was later sold to Viacom. Gwen Baker became an internationally known educator, while Andrea Roane, a news anchor, is widely respected throughout the Washington, D.C., metropolitan area.

This group is profiled first in the section titled *Women Who Made it Big.* The next section, *Educators Making a Difference,* provides a snapshot of women who remained in that field throughout their career. Some, like Gail Nordmoe and Iris Metts, rose from classroom teacher to the superintendent level. Also, Rachel Petty and Deagelia Pena describe their experiences becoming university administrators and beyond. Finally, the last section highlights the career moves of three *Women to Watch.* Medical doctor Beatrice Muglia and newspaper publisher Joy Bramble shed light on their career paths, and Rondalyn Kane describes the preparation she had before accepting a Presidential appointment in the U.S. Department of Labor.

This range of career choices provides a glimpse of what it took for these women to move up in their chosen career and become the influential women they are today.

While reading the stories of these 14 minority women, you will notice some similarities and remarkable differences in their backgrounds, accomplishments, and dreams for themselves. Some set out on one career path, only to change it at the most unexpected time. Some endured remarkable hardship and still thrived. Others stayed in their chosen fields even while moving around the country with their children. Ten of the 14 women profiled here had children. An almost equal number—nine—were single or divorced.

The portraits in this chapter show that intellectual achievement was just as important to these women as their financial achievements. Many of the women earned multiple college degrees, including bachelor's, master's, and doctoral degrees. Some who had attended college were subsequently awarded honorary doctoral degrees based on their tremendous performance in their chosen career fields.

Ultimately, I hope that these women's stories will shape your ideas and inform your decisions when choosing your own career. Besides my own original research, I have used secondary sources for some of the well-known women, when available, to give you a broader account of the events occurring in the lives of these women. Now, let the journey began.

WOMEN WHO MADE IT BIG

Cathy Hughes—"A Lesson in Perseverance"
Founder and Chairperson of Radio One, TV One Executive

In 1980, Cathy Hughes recalled that she was sleeping on the floor of her recently acquired radio station, WOL-AM.[1] Her radio company was not profitable, which resulted in extreme financial hardship for her. According to many published interviews, her second marriage to Dewey Hughes, a broadcast journalist, ended shortly after the purchase.[2] Hughes realized that her decision would come at a great personal cost to her, and she found herself losing her apartment and living in her radio station. When she lost her car to repossession, she told reporters, "I watched them jack it up and drive it away. I thought, there's not much more."[3]

It is likely that someone with less stamina would have given up on her dreams of getting into broadcasting. Here was a woman who was rejected 32 times for a business loan. She told reporter Johnnie Roberts that she, Dewey, and others had to come up with $100,000 and seek other investors in order to secure a $500,000 loan on her 33rd try.[4] Shortly after that tremendous success, she and Dewey divorced, but she would still have to make payments on the $1 million loan that would become due. In addition to living at the station and suffering other indignities, she had very little money to pay on that loan. She told an *Ebony* magazine reporter that she sent what she could to satisfy her bill collectors.[5] In that same article, she said that she sold a rare white gold pocket watch that belonged to her great grandmother, a former slave, for $50,000, to save her business.

Aside from her many financial difficulties, she had to raise her son, Alfred Liggins III, now CEO of her broadcast empire, alone. Hughes was well acquainted with the rigors of being a single mother since she had given birth to Alfred at 16, according to interviewer Johnnie Roberts.[6] Although she had later married her childhood sweetheart, Alfred Liggins, the marriage lasted for only two years. Now with her second husband gone, she again had the sole responsibility of juggling parenthood and her radio business activities.

She found a solution to some of her work and family challenges by taking little Alfred along on her business dealings. She told *Ebony* reporter Norment,

"I bought him his first tux at age eight and he used to go to all these black tie events with me. I made it clear that it was either Alfred and me or no me. I would not sacrifice the time I would spend with him. I was not letting the city raise my son."[7] How did this arrangement work out for her? "My work was wonderful because I was there 24/7," Hughes said.[8] In this sense her experience differed from other mothers who have chosen to work outside of the home and who typically must juggle their family responsibilities around the eight-hour time period that they spend working for their employer.

Even in such dire financial circumstances, Cathy persevered and never gave up on her broadcasting dreams. By 1986 the company began making a profit, and by 1987 Hughes was able to pay $7.5 million for a second radio station in Washington, D.C., WMMJ-FM (Majic 102.3), which had a contemporary urban format. Regarding that purchase, Hughes said she did not believe her company would have survived if she had not been able to give her WOL (AM) radio station an FM big sister.[9] That is, Hughes wanted to diversify her radio ownership so she could be more competitive in gaining radio ads with multiple stations versus owning only a single station. Within a decade, Hughes had acquired seven other radio stations. By May 1999, she and her son Alfred took the company public, making her the first African-American woman with a company on the New York Stock Exchange. In 2004, she acquired a 51 percent share in Reach Media, and during that same year she started a new cable television station, TV One, with Comcast as a partner. TV One is designed to focus on African-American lifestyles and offers syndicated and original programming, gospel music, and interviews conducted by Hughes herself in the show *TV One on One.* Hughes has interviewed a host of celebrities (Kenneth Babyface Edmonds, Chris Rock) and politicians (Senators Barack Obama and Hillary Clinton, Congressman Charles Rangel).

According to the March 1, 2008, Standard & Poor's stock report, the company that Hughes founded, Radio One, Inc., had estimated revenue of $330.3 million in 2007.[10] The company owns or operates 70 stations in 22 markets, and its total net worth has been valued at over $2 billion.

But now Cathy must deal with her next challenge. The company's stock shares plunged to a low of $1.26 in 2008, which represents a huge drop from its debut at $24 a share in 1999 to a rise of $97 a share in 2000. Nevertheless, the 2008 Standard & Poor stock analysts indicate that "Radio One, Inc. has historically outpaced overall industry growth due, in our opinion, to its growing urban market niche."[11] Hughes and other company principals, including her son Alfred, have noted in various public reports that it will address various management issues and difficulties encountered in some of their radio markets, such as Los Angeles. The company has hired a new chief financial officer and is reorganizing or selling some of the less-profitable stations. Those types of steps have led Standard & Poor's analysts to believe that " these measures could start to bear fruit in late 2008."[12] They believe the company's TV One cable venture will potentially benefit the parent company as well. It is just that kind of confidence that will likely propel the woman dubbed variously as one of the "100 Most Powerful," "100 Most Influential," or "100 Who Have Changed the World" (by *Washingtonian, Regardies,* and *Essence* magazines, respectively) to turn her company's stock price around. She has also been called one of the "10 Most Powerful Women in Black America," and *Black Enterprise* named her one of the "50 Most Powerful Women in Business" in 2006.

Hughes has taken college courses in business administration at Creighton University and the University of Nebraska. As a result of her phenomenal success in both business and in giving back to the community, she told me that she has received honorary doctoral degrees from universities such as Howard and Southeastern in Washington, D.C. and Syracuse University in New York.

In 2005, the Department of Radio, Television and Film School at Howard University named her the newest Time Warner Endowed Chair, which was established as a result of a $2 million grant from the Time Warner Corporation in 1999. Previous influential recipients have included film director and actor Bill Duke and chairman and CEO of de Passe Entertainment, Suzanne de Passe.

Hughes has received numerous local and national awards, far too many to list. They include the Lifetime Achievement Award from the Washington Area Broadcasters Association, the National Association of Broadcasters Distinguished Service Awards, the Seventh Congressional District Humanitarian Award, the Lifetime Achievement Award from the National Association of Black Broadcasters, and the Maryland Chamber of Commerce Business Hall of Fame.

With all of her success, Hughes has never forgotten her modest upbringing. The advice she shares in later chapters of this book demonstrates one of her memorable mottos that she lives by: "Your attitude determines your altitude." She is determined to bring more African-Americans into management, ownership, on-air, and sales opportunities. By 2005, her company employed about 1,500 black broadcasters at Radio One. When asked whether, if she could start over, she would choose the same line of professional work, Hughes said, "Yes, I absolutely love radio. It's a lot easier to do a job that you love to do."

Debra Lee—"Risk Taker Par Excellence"
Chairman and Chief Executive Officer of Black Entertainment Television Networks

Debra Lee can be described as a risk taker. While most of the 14 women that I interviewed for this project have made some risky decisions in their climb to the top, Lee's decision to leave Steptoe and Johnson, a highly acclaimed law firm in Washington, D.C. that employed more than 200 lawyers, for an entertainment company that didn't have a legal department raised more than a few eyebrows. You will learn how this single decision led to her amazing journey within the Black Entertainment Television (BET) ranks.

Lee is probably best known for her work in several senior positions at the BET, including taking over the number-one position from the company's founder, billionaire business executive Robert Johnson. Lee's career at the cable network began in 1986, when she was hired as vice president and general counsel. She rose quickly through the BET ranks holding such positions as executive vice president and general counsel, then president and chief operating officer in 1996, and finally the top spot as president and chief executive officer in June 2005. In a news release to the media, the company quoted then CEO Bob Johnson as saying, "I could not have chosen a better chief executive and outstanding leader to succeed me at BET than Debra Lee, and that's what makes this announcement so important to me and positive for BET's future. Few executives in this industry have exhibited the ability to manage a unique growth company and shown the commitment to building a successful brand the way Debra has in her 19 years at BET. She mastered the cable programming industry long ago and has a strong executive team in place to support her as she leads BET within the Viacom family."[13] Johnson had indicated that he planned to retire from the company by January 2006. Lee would begin a new chapter in her career as chairman and CEO when Johnson left.

During Lee's tenure, BET saw steady increases in its revenue. She is widely credited with being a major force in getting the company on the New York Stock Exchange in 1991. At that time, the company's stock rose from $17 at its initial offering to about $60 prior to being sold to Viacom. She told a *Billboard* magazine reporter in 2005 that BET was the "first African-American company to be traded publicly on the New York Stock Exchange. We went private in 1998 and the company was acquired by Viacom in 2000."[14] Since then, BET continues to show huge revenue increases under her leadership at Viacom. For example, in 2007 Umstead reported that BET saw its revenue rise from $231 million in 2001 to $494 million in 2006.[15]

BET Founder Robert Johnson sold the company to Viacom for a whopping $3 billion, a move that allowed Debra Lee and a number of other workplace colleagues to join the millionaire ranks and enabled Lee to exercise her management skills further by presiding over BET Networks. Also, that move placed Lee in company with other top women in charge of some of Viacom's best-known brands, including Judy McGrath, chairman and CEO of MTV Networks; Cyma Zarghami, president of Nickelodeon/MTVN Kids and Family Group, and Gay Berman, president of Paramount Pictures.

In 2006, Lee told *Fortune* magazine writer Patricia Sellers that her smartest career decision was joining BET. "I was at a corporate law firm in D.C.," she said. "We didn't have cable yet. BET was a client—a six-year-old company with 80 employees and just 10 million subscribers. The partners in my law firm said, 'What? You're going where?' I remember being told that I was stepping off the fast track. But I believed in the mission. I had grown up with brands like Ebony and Motown and I grew up in the segregated South in Greensboro, so a black-owned business was really important to me."[16]

Lee took a monumental risk to leave the well-known firm of Steptoe and Johnson to move to BET, a startup company. Things could have taken a different turn and landed Lee in a situation that her former colleagues had imagined—moving off of the fast track. In February 2007, she told a group of students at her alma mater, Brown University, "no one thought I would last as (BET's) first full-time, in-house lawyer. Given cable television's then murky future, the career move was risky."[17] However, in that same interview with *Fortune* magazine, Lee recalls growing up in an army family and moving around a great deal, which apparently prepared her for some risk taking. "My dad never set boundaries for me as a girl. When I moved to Greensboro, North Carolina, in the sixth grade, they elected me class president because no one else wanted it. It was a terrifying experience but it set the tone for the rest of my life."[18] Indeed, when I asked her in a much-earlier interview at what point in her life she became aware of her desire to be successful, Lee said that she seemed to always manage to work in leadership positions. She recalled working hard for success in the sixth grade, too, in college at Brown University, and later in her work at Harvard Law School.

Despite all of her success, being in such a visible and high-powered position at BET has made her the target of some critics, who bemoan the cable channel's portrayal of women in the music videos it airs. Lee reminds her critics that the company appeals to the 18–34 age group. Moreover, she points out that she is actively planning to add more original programming to address some of the critics' concerns. For example, in a September 2007 *Broadcasting and Cable* special report, David Goetzl discusses the original series launched during the summer of 2007 and the shows undertaken under the leadership of Reginald Hudlin, a well-known Hollywood producer hired in 2005 to serve as entertainment president.[19] That lineup includes a gospel competition show, *Bufu,* a spin-off of reality series *College Hill,* a court show, *Judge Mooney,* animated shows, BET's first scripted comedy show, and a town hall-style show on the complexities of hip hop music. Whether the introduction of this new programming will reduce the number of BET critics remains to be seen.

Debra Lee, at age 54, is a regular recipient of a host of prestigious awards, both within her industry and in the community. Among her awards is the National Cable and Telecommunication Association Distinguished Vanguard Award for Leadership in 2003. In 2001, she received the Woman of the Year Award from the Women in Cable and Telecommunications. In 2000, she received the Tower of Power Trumpet Award from Turner Broadcasting and was recognized as one of the Hundred Heavy Hitters in Cable by Fox Magazine. In 2005, the Congressional Black Caucus Foundation recognized her with its Phoenix Award for significant contributions to society. Also in 2005, she received the Madame C. J. Walker Award from *Ebony* magazine for bringing the entrepreneurial spirit of the pioneering black businesswoman in 2005.

Lee has been active outside of her job at BET, too. She serves on the board of directors of Eastman Kodak Company; the Kennedy Center's Community and Friends Board, the Alvin Ailey Dance Theater, Girls Inc., The Marriott Corporation, and Revlon Corporation, to name a few. She is also a trustee emeritus at Brown University,

At the time of my interview Lee was married. Now, she is a single mother with two children, adding even more responsibilities to her busy day-to-day schedule. Lee expects to continue to take BET Networks, now under the umbrella of Viacom, to even greater heights. From this portrait of Lee, you can see that she likely will not mind taking more risk to do so.

Eunice Dudley—"It's A Family Affair"
Chief Financial Officer of Dudley Products

Eunice Dudley admits that she did not start off so focused. As a teenager, she told me, "I wanted to be a psychiatrist. I wanted to work with juvenile delinquents." Her mother, Eva Murdock Mosley (now deceased), was a teacher who, with her minister father, Andrew Mosley Sr., raised Eunice with eight other siblings in Selma, Alabama.

Eunice recalls that she enjoyed her childhood as the seventh of nine children. She remembers having a garden at home in the country. "I was one of the youngest, so I had the easiest job—to water plants." Also, she fondly recalled staying very busy at school and participating in numerous outside activities. She played basketball, the trombone, the piano, and the organ, and she was a majorette. She said she attended church conventions most summers.

The orderliness took a different turn for her, however, when she entered college. "College was tough my first year. It was a rude awakening," she told me. "I was one of thousands and there was no one there to monitor what you were doing." In other words, gone were the supervisory eyes of her older siblings. She realized that she would have to become more focused in order to do better in her college studies.

Eunice decided to take a job selling Fuller hair care products during the summer of 1960. She found out about the job from her aunt and uncle who worked for the company, and who lived in New York. That decision would change her career path. She took the job to earn some money for her college tuition, and in doing so she eventually met Joe Dudley Sr., who was selling Fuller products too. Both were pursuing their college studies at the time, but within a year the two were married in 1961.

No longer interested in psychiatry, Eunice decided in 1962 to work full time for Fuller Products along with her husband. That partnership never ended. She credits Mr. Fuller with teaching her and her husband the product sales business. The two eventually started their own business, Dudley Products, after realizing how successful they could be in business for themselves. What began as a startup, manufacturing products in their kitchen, with Eunice and her kids packaging the products at night and Joe leading the sales team by day, eventually became a multimillion-dollar hair care and cosmetic company. Now they have a sales force of over 400 representatives and sales of over $50 million, according to the company's Dun & Bradstreet report.[20]

Today, Eunice and Joe are joined by their three adult children in managing the business. The company includes several other businesses—Dudley Inn, Dudley Cafeteria, a travel agency, and the Dudley Cosmetology University, which has offices in Chicago; Washington, D.C.; and Charlotte, Durham, and Kernerville, North Carolina. Their son, Joe Jr., is vice president of finance for Dudley Products. Ursula is director and vice president of marketing of Dudley Cosmetics. Genea, their youngest daughter, is a brand manager in the marketing department of the company.

Like Cathy Hughes and Debra Lee, Eunice has a long list of awards and recognitions. Bennett College bestowed the Honorary Doctor of Humane Letters Degree upon her for her business success. In addition, she received the Crystal Award from the National Association of Negro Business Women's Clubs Inc., the Kernerville's First Citizen of the Year Award, and the Athena Award from the Greensboro Chamber of Commerce.

Eunice's community work has taken her abroad on many occasions. She served as a committee member for organizing the School of Management for Africa University, located in Muture, Zimbabwe, Africa. She and company leaders are working on developing other cosmetology programs for Brazil and other Caribbean countries.

Although Eunice attended Talladega University with dreams of becoming a psychiatrist, she said that if she could start over she would choose the same line of professional work that she has now. "I learned so much from business—understanding all of the office operations," she told me. Apparently she and husband Joe learned a great deal together from their chance meeting selling Fuller Products. It really became a family affair for them.

Zina Pierre—"From Homecoming Queen to the White House"
President of Washington Linkage Group

Zina Pierre had big dreams as a kid. "I had this attitude growing up that I could do anything that I wanted to do. I wrote a lot of poetry at seven. I was very well liked in school. I was named homecoming queen for my school," she recalled to me.

Pierre was among the three youngest women that I interviewed. At the time of her interview, she was a special assistant for intergovernmental affairs to President Bill Clinton. Zina was born in 1967, the daughter of a nurse and a military father who joined the teaching ranks after retirement. Since her parents separated when she was young, she credits one of her cousins as taking on the mother role for her from the time she was 15 until her college days.

Pierre believes that she was blessed with a focused mind. Even in junior high school she knew she wanted to be a writer or a reporter. She told me she wanted to be in the communications field because she earned good grades in English and history. She would later go on to work at Gannett as a receptionist. "Some people thought that this was a downgrade for me but they did not realize that I would be working in the presidential suite of the company," she said. "These would be the people who could help me get to my next job. I would be in a position to meet the right people since my face would be the first one they saw before meeting the president of the company."

Her political savvy served Pierre well, and she began working in the federal government after Clinton was elected. Starting out as a speechwriter, she later moved on to the Department of Labor as a director of Communications. From there she took a job as director of the Small Business Administration's Initiative on Welfare to Work. By 2000, she landed her position in the White House, becoming the second-highest-ranking African American there.

As special assistant to President Bill Clinton for Intergovernmental Affairs, Pierre dealt with an array of policy issues, including the Digital Divide, Health Care, Census 2000, International Trade and Empowerment Zone, and Enterprise Community Initiatives. She also had the distinct honor of serving on the Presidential-appointed Council of Advisors for restoring the town of Princeville, North Carolina, the oldest black-owned town in the United States.

Pierre's honors in business and in the community are substantial. She is listed in the Black History Makers Hall of Fame, and the Minority Business Suppliers named her Outstanding Government Official of the Year. She received Outstanding Service Recognition by the National Conference of Mayors and is a three-time recipient of Vice President Gore's Heroes of Reinvention Award. She is also listed in Who's Who in the World and Who's Who in Business.

Her community activities include service on the board of a number of political and civic organizations. She is currently vice chair of the "Future Pac," a national African-American women's political action committee. She has served as a board member of the Greater Washington Urban League, the Black Women's Roundtable, and the Women's Vote Center of the Democratic National Committee, and she has worked with the Annapolis Children and Family Service Department. In business since leaving the Clinton Administration, Pierre is now president and CEO of the Washington Linkage Group, which specializes in lobbying, public relations, and international trade issues. She is an ordained minister as well.

Pierre's educational credentials include a bachelor's degree from the Catholic University of America and a Master's of Divinity Degree from Howard University. It seems that her belief that she could do anything that she wanted to do from an early age certainly served her well in making her career choices.

Andrea Roane—"Stayed at the Right Place"
Washington, D.C., News Anchor

Andrea Roane, the daughter of an Illinois Central Railroad station manager and an elementary school teacher, still remembers some of the first jobs that brought her into the workforce. "I worked in a commercial for Popeye's, and I was also an extra in a James Bond movie," she recalled. She told me the wait for the part was really long, but she found it to be fascinating.

As a teenager, Roane wanted to be a teacher like her mother. She studied speech at the Louisiana State University in New Orleans (now University of New Orleans), obtaining both a bachelor's and a master's degree there. Although Roane did get the opportunity to teach English in middle and high school, her teaching career was short lived. She became an educational reporter for a public TV station, WYES, in New Orleans in 1975. That career switch set her on the path to broadcast journalism. Andrea told me that "all of my early jobs were a training ground for what I do now as a TV anchor."

That training ground had earned her the label of "one of the most trusted and recognizable journalists in Washington, D.C. news" by her employer, 9 Eyewitness News. Over the years, she coanchored the 4 pm, 6 pm, and 11 pm newscasts. Today she has come full circle back to the morning slots where she first began, although they are now at 5 am, 6 am, and 9 am.

Some of the most surprising moves at the station came when management assigned her to replace one of the veteran reporters, Maureen Bunyan, another well-known black female anchor. Bunyan, a Columbia University graduate, left the station in 1995 due to a contract dispute with management. Andrea coanchored the 6 pm and 11 pm newscasts for five years until 2000 before being replaced by a younger minority woman anchor who has since left the station for a rival station.

When I interviewed Roane, she was adamant that if she had to start over again, she would stay in the same line of professional work that she is in now. "I would not change anything," she said. "I have a very good life, a good family, and a very good upbringing." However, she admitted that her biggest difficulty at Channel 9 was with the new management trying to decide what to do. "I really don't have a struggle story," she added. However, the constant assignments to different news slots may be seen as a struggle considering the disruptions that it can cause to one's life, especially to a mother raising children.

Later in a 2006 interview with a Washington, D.C. reporter concerning her longevity with the Channel 9 television station, she characterized her time there as being similar to the demands of a reality TV show—"survivor," "outwit," "outplay," and "outlast."[21] Her longevity with the Channel 9 station allowed her to cover major local and national community leaders, entertainers, and politicians. That list includes Archbishop Desmond Tutu, author Mary Higgins Clarke, former Defense Secretary William Cohen, and Magic Johnson, to name a few.

Roane's work in the health care area fighting breast cancer shows her passion for saving lives in the community as well. According to her most recent news profile, thousands of Washington-area women have signed on to her breast cancer awareness program, Buddy Check 9.

A three-time Emmy award-winning anchor, Roane added Georgetown University's 2004 Lombardi Symbol of Caring Award to her list of recognitions. That award is given to someone "who makes extraordinary strides in emerging cancer research, prevention and treatment through awareness and philanthropy." Her other community work includes serving as cochair of the Kennedy Center Community and Friends Board and board member of the National Museum of Women in the Arts. She serves as a member of the Cancer Research and Prevention Foundation and the Howard University Hospital Cancer Advisory Board.

Her many awards include 2006 Washingtonian of the Year, the Media Excellence Award from the National Foundation of Women Legislators, the National Figure/Outstanding Person from the Catholic Youth Organization, the Outstanding Community Commitment Award from the Columbia Hospital for Women, the Susan B. Anthony Award for Community Service from the National Organization of Women, the Innovators in Advocacy Award from the George Washington University, and the Women of Distinction Award from the Northern Seaboard Region and Greater Washington Area Chapter of Hadassah.

Roane's staying power with Channel 9 News has proven quite lucrative for her as she celebrates 28 years with the station this year. Back in 2000, she revealed that her salary was in the $300,00 to $499,000 range. From that alone, it is easy to see that she has indeed surpassed her childhood dreams of "wanting to live well and not scrimp," as she put it to me.

Roane is married with two adult children.

Jane Smith—"Visionary Leader"
Executive Director, Spelman College Center for Leadership & Civic Engagement

"I had visions of leading, speaking, and being in charge, just like my grand-mother," Jane Smith told me in an interview. She remembers feeling this way since she was about five years old and said that somehow she knew she was privi-leged. As her story will reveal, that was indeed the case.

Smith was born in Atlanta in 1946, surrounded by a number of family firsts. Her father was one of the first black dentists in Atlanta, and her mother was a public school teacher. Her grandmother was the first black superintendent of an all-black school district. "Grandmother had an office in City Hall," she recalled, adding that her grandmother was a student of the noted scholar W. E. B. Du Bois, the first black to graduate from Harvard University. With so many accomplished family members around her, it is not surprising that young Jane believed that she would be in charge too.

When Smith was a teenager, she wanted to be a lawyer. "I wanted to be the first black Perry Mason," she said. However, it was her coursework at Spelman College, one of the leading historically black colleges for women, that fueled her desire toward the nonprofit sector, where she ultimately worked for several decades. For example, she worked as the managing director for INROADS/Atlanta and INROADS/Detroit (two career-development programs) from 1981 to 1990. In addition, she raised funds for the Martin Luther King Center for Nonviolent Social Change, after accepting an invitation from Mrs. Coretta Scott King to become the organization's director of Development. After her exemplary work on President Jimmy's Carter's Atlanta Project, aimed at reducing poverty in poor neighborhoods, she caught the attention of Dr. Dorothy Height, President Emeritus and Board Chairwoman of the National Council of Negro Women (NCNW), in Dr. Height's search for a successor.

According to a February 1998 article in the *Atlanta Journal-Constitution*, Dr. Height said, "One of the appealing things about Smith is she has the broad view, but she also has a demonstrated ability to work with people at improving people's lives."[22] In that same interview, Dr. Height mentioned Smith's work with the King Center and The Atlanta Project. Additionally, others who where interviewed said "her vision as well as her ability to manage change, forge collaboration and work under such a prominent figure as former President Jimmy Carter helped her secure the top spot at the National Council of Negro Women."[23]

After serving for three years as the president and CEO of the NCNW, Smith found herself moving on to work for another large women's organization. This time she, too, became a first: the first black chief executive officer of the Business and Professional Women/USA, an organization with more than 30,000 members when she took over.

Today, Smith has returned to her Atlanta roots. She is the executive director of the Center for Leadership and Civic Engagement at her alma mater, Spelman College. One of the major goals of the center is to become a premier empowerment center for women of color. Smith is indeed the woman to make this happen given her experience leading national women's organizations, her vast network of contacts, and her fund-raising abilities. While at the NCNW, she managed an $11.5-million annual budget, a staff of 50, and thousands of volunteers.

Jane is the recipient of numerous awards. She received honorary doctorates from Spelman College and Texas College, and *Success Guide* recognized her as one of America's 50 Most Influential Black Speakers. *Life, Essence, Ebony,* and *Ms.* magazines have featured her accomplishments. She is further profiled in *Notable Black American Women.*

Over her career, Smith was appointed to numerous high-level commissions, boards, and national organizations. For example, she has served on the Board of Bank America (then called the Citizen and Southern Bank) and Leadership Atlanta. President Clinton appointed her to the National Women's Business Council, and former Secretary of State Madeline K. Albright chose her as a delegate to the United Nations Beijing Plus Five Conference.

Smith received a Bachelor of Arts degree in Sociology from Spelman College. She earned her Master's Degree in Sociology from Emory University and received her Ph.D. in Education from Harvard University.

The young girl who knew she was privileged has done a great deal and has utilized her vast talent to improve the lives of countless others in this country and abroad.

Gwendolyn Calvert Baker—"An International Voice for Children"
Former President of UNICEF

A native of Ann Arbor, Michigan, and the daughter of a factory worker and a beautician, Gwendolyn Calvert Baker told me that as a young child she knew she wanted to be a teacher and a leader. She saw herself leading a class of imaginary children and teaching them. These ideas stayed with her throughout her teenage years, too.

Born in 1931 at a time when occupational choices were quite limited for blacks, she knew that at least teaching was a viable option for her. Her grandmother, her teachers, her dentist, and others around her wanted her to go to college. Although she went to schools that were predominantly white, Calvert Baker did not mention any problems with prejudice there.

She attended college but dropped out at 18 to get married. She put her college studies on hold to raise her children. It was not until she was in her thirties that she obtained her Bachelor's of Art degree in Elementary Education from the University of Michigan in 1964.

Armed with her bachelor's degree, Calvert Baker realized her teaching dreams by accepting a job with the public schools in Ann Arbor, Michigan. Her next goal was to become a principal at her school, but things were about to take a different twist for her. During her third year of teaching in public schools, she decided to pursue a master's degree. She left the public school system to join the faculty at her alma mater and later obtained a Ph.D. degree. Her success as a tenured associate professor eventually led her to take an administrative position as director of affirmative action at the University of Michigan.

After two years, Calvert Baker found herself spreading her wings to take high-level positions in Washington, D.C. and New York City. She served as chief of the Minorities and Women's Program at the National Institute of Education in Washington, and from that position she moved on to hold other executive positions. They included vice president and dean for Graduate and Children's

Program at Bank Street College of Education in New York City, national executive director of the YWCA of the U.S.A., and then president and chief executive officer at the United States Committee for the United Nations Children's Educational Fund (UNICEF).

Calvert Baker's positions with the YWCA and UNICEF allowed her to use her expertise serving as a spokesperson, fund raiser, and implementer of policies and programs in order to better use the organizations' resources nationwide and abroad. During her nine years with the YWCA, she traveled to more than 16 countries on official business, including Thailand, Hong Kong, Japan, Nairobi, London, France, Switzerland, and El Salvador. With UNICEF, she traveled to member African countries, including Mozambique, Uganda, Nigeria, Ghana, Cameron, and Ethiopia, to name a few.

In addition, she has an extensive record of research and community service. She has published books, articles in scholarly journals and the popular press, and chapters in educational books. Her books include *Planning and Organizing for Multicultural Instruction,* published by Addison Wesley, and *Redesigning the Nonprofit Organization* for the National Center for Nonprofit Boards. She has also served with distinction on numerous boards, councils, and commissions throughout her career. One of her most notable accomplishments was serving simultaneously on the New York City Board of Education while working with the YWCA. As a member and later president of the Board, she oversaw the management and operation of a district that served nearly one million students.

Not surprisingly, Calvert Baker has received many honors and awards. The University of Michigan, Chicago State University, Bentley College, Fairleigh Dickinson University, Medgar Evers College of the City University of New York, King College, and Southeastern Massachusetts University all have awarded her honorary doctorate degrees. The Congressman Augustus Hawkins Education Service Award, the Trailblazer of the Year, and the Leadership for the Rights of Children are just a few of the 40 awards that she received from women's, civic, and educational organizations across the nation.

Although she told me that she wanted to be in finance and may have pursued an MBA if the doors were open back then, Calvert Baker has no regrets about her career path. She received all of her degrees—bachelors, masters, and Ph.D.—from the University of Michigan. The educational community seems to be quite fortunate for the tireless energy, productivity, and indelible imprints that she made in the educational field.

OTHER WOMEN WHO CHOSE EDUCATION CAREERS

The next four women elected to pursue terminal degrees in the field of education. They acquired either the coveted educational doctorate (Ed.D.) or doctor of philosophy (Ph.D.). Unlike some of their colleagues that you have already met, these women chose to stay in the educational field throughout their careers.

Iris Metts—"A Leader in Public Education"
Former Superintendent, Prince George's County, Maryland

Iris Metts devoted almost 40 years of her career to improving educational outcomes for public schools in Virginia, Illinois, Delaware, and Maryland. Beginning in 1964 as a physics and mathematics instructor at Armstrong High School in Richmond, Virginia, she moved through the school system ranks at various locations. She held positions from principal and assistant superintendent to superintendent of schools. At the superintendent level, she led the Christina School District of Newark, Delaware, and the Prince George's County Public School System in Maryland.

Before coming to the 132,000 Prince George's County School system, she was appointed by the governor of Delaware to be the state's first Secretary of Education. She held the top job in Delaware for two years. Her tenure in the top job in Prince George's County lasted for three years from 1999 to 2003.

When I interviewed then Superintendent Metts, she told me that as a teenager she wanted to be a teacher. She accomplished that goal, and so much more. She believes that her appointments to the top jobs have led the way for more minority women to be considered for such high-profile jobs. In addition, she recalled that in Delaware, many of the conservatives were astonished that the governor would appoint a black person to be that state's Secretary of Education. "I had one of the longest Senate confirmations," she said. "I have led the way for others who will come behind me."

Iris's tenure with the Prince George's County System is probably one of the few times that she encountered the most public adversity of her professional career. Employed by a school board that was later viewed as dysfunctional, she experienced her first firing from a job. She was promptly reinstated on appeal. The Maryland General Assembly approved legislation disbanding the existing school board, and it gave the governor of Maryland and the Prince George's County Executive the power to appoint members of their choice to the newly formed school board.

"I have never been fired before in my life," she said. Still, with her job restored, she managed to continue implementing many new school improvements for the county's public schools. Student achievement test scores improved under her leadership, and she earned between $200,000 and $249,000 for her expertise at the time.

Her next employer, Mosaica Education, cited her many accomplishments in the Prince George's County Public School System, crediting her with the introduction of a full-day of kindergarten program and mandatory summer school programs for those needing help and for implementing class-size reductions and establishing the first public military academy in Maryland.[24]

Numerous organizations and groups have recognized Metts for her academic accomplishments, leadership, and community work. They include Delaware

Superintendent of the Year, the Distinguished Leadership Award from the American Association of University of Women Newark Branch, and the Newark NAACP's Outstanding Community Service Martin Luther King Dinner Award. The Greater Washington Board of Trade awarded her its Outstanding Service Leadership in Public Service. Her vast community activities include serving as a member of the National Commission on Mathematics and Science and Teaching for the 21st Century. She is also a board member of the Horace Mann League, the Delaware Native Society, and the Mid-Atlantic Laboratory for Student Success.

Metts's preparation for securing the superintendent jobs she held around the country includes acquiring three degrees. She received a Bachelors of Science in Physics and Mathematics from Hampton University in 1964, a Masters of Arts degree in Physics and Mathematics from the College of William and Mary in 1971, and a doctorate in Education Administration from the Virginia Polytechnic and State University in 1982. She completed postdoctoral work at Harvard University.

Metts continues her passion for the education of children as the president and CEO of her own company, A+ Solutions Inc. When I asked her if she would choose the same line of professional work, she said, "Yes, I have no doubts about my choices."

As the daughter of a factory foreman and barber and whose mother was employed in the nursing field, Metts found that being a "bit of a bookworm in college" reaped great benefits for her and the many students whose lives she improved.

Rachel Petty—"Found Career/ Family Balance"
Dean of the College of Arts and Sciences, University of the District of Columbia

If I told you that every summer since the 10th grade and during her college years, Rachel Petty worked in her aunt and uncle's bank, you might think that her career interests would be in financial services. Wrong. Rachel told me that even though she liked working with numbers and liked that it was an African American-owned business, she wanted to be a teacher.

Born in 1941 in Columbia, South Carolina, Petty said she enjoyed her childhood days with her two brothers and two sisters. Her mother was a teacher and her father was a brick mason. "My parents created a lot of opportunities for us," she told me. Aside from her mother, she said, "My ninth grade teacher inspired me."

After obtaining her bachelor's degree from Howard University in Washington, D.C., in 1964, Petty received her master's and doctorate degrees from the University of Maryland in 1968 and 1980, respectively. "I enjoyed my college years, but I was not really that social. I just worked hard," she recalled.

Petty joined academia as an adjunct lecturer in the Department of Education at Howard University from 1968 to 1971. She became an instructor at the University of the District of Columbia in the Department of Psychology in 1971.

Over the years, she moved up the hierarchy, holding each subsequent position leading to her current position as dean of the College of Arts and Sciences. In other words, Rachel moved from assistant professor, to associate professor, to professor, chairperson of the Psychology Department, assistant dean, acting dean, and, finally, the coveted Dean position. This type of progression is not unusual for those who want to move up in academia. There may be cases when some employees move faster by skipping over some of the ranks. Typically, this might depend on your other professional contacts both within and outside of the university community.

Petty pointed out to me that she was the only African-American woman to occupy the dean position. For the most part, she told me, "There is a male-dominated culture. There seems to be a club where men think they should be in power. Reaching this position did not come easily for me," she said. Her point here should be underscored. The previous occupants of the dean's office included two white men, a white woman, and an African man. In addition, Rachel had about 30 years of senior-level experience in teaching and administration before obtaining the dean's job.

The National Association for Equal Opportunity in Higher Education, the *International Who's Who in American Women,* the *Who's Who Among African Americans,* and the Psi Chi Honorary Society in Psychology are among those recognizing her contributions in the field of psychology.

Petty's love for the well being of children has been demonstrated by her long-time commitment to various community activities. For example, she served on the Maryland Foster Care Review Board. In addition, she has worked with the Lutheran Social Services of the National Capitol Area and the District of Columbia Child Welfare Consortium.

Rachel's career path demonstrates so clearly that it can be a lengthy period of time before one can rise to some of the top positions in academia. She succinctly points out, too, that one may face a fair share of obstacles like the ones she encountered. Nevertheless, she found her career path to be quite fulfilling.

"I would not change my career path if I had to start all over again. Because of my socialization, I needed to be able to have a career that would allow me to be at home and do things with my children," she said. Petty is married with two adult children.

Gail Nordmoe—"Kept Walking Toward Success"
Former Assistant Superintendent, Cambridge Public Schools, Cambridge, Massachusetts

What had Gail Nordmoe and her male classmate done to some of the students at another local high school to encounter racial slurs and to be told to go home? After all, she and her male classmate and her teacher were only there to participate in the science fair. She told me, "My teacher reacted quickly by telling us to keep on walking and hold our heads high." Not only did she and her classmate keep walking, they both won first place in the categories that they entered at the science fair.

That memory served as a reminder to Nordmoe of how far our country still has to go to resolve some of the ugly prejudices that have plagued our nation. "Winning my award kept me from dwelling on this painful encounter," she told me.

Nordmoe grew up in a close-knit family as the daughter of a blue-collar worker and a homemaker. She had one sister, and said her childhood was really nice. "I skipped the second grade and part of the sixth grade. I remember receiving the outstanding student award for the whole elementary school," she said. She was an honor roll student continually and graduated from high school in three and a half years.

"High school was the most fun for me. I was vice president of my senior class, participated in lots of extracurricular activities, and I was voted 'most likely to succeed in school,' " Nordmoe revealed. Given all of this, she said she knew prejudice existed, but "I had never felt it like I did at the science fair." Nevertheless, she did not let that incident sway her from achieving at high levels.

Nordmoe recalled that her experiences in college were less positive. "I found college to be very difficult," she said of the years she attended the University of Illinois on a full scholarship. "This is one of the Big Ten schools that was highly segregated in 1960. There were very few African Americans in the school of about 27,000," she recalled. This was quite an experience for a young woman who had attended the same all-black high school as her mother and aunt.

Although during her high school years Gail was interested in the sciences and wanted to be a pharmacist, her interest changed in college. She majored in sociology and minored in history.

After graduating from the University of Illinois in 1963, she accepted a position teaching in the Chicago public school system. From there Nordmoe moved to the Detroit public school system, where she held various positions such as principal and assistant director over a 20-year period.

One of the highlights of her career came when she was invited to join the Danbury, Connecticut, public schools as the assistant superintendent for curriculum and instruction. That position brought a substantial salary increase and "offered new challenges for me," she said. Although Danbury was a small school system, the diversity there was tremendous. "I found students speaking over 43 different languages representing over 60 countries," she said.

Nordmoe remained flexible in her career choices by subsequently taking on three new opportunities. She worked as an assistant superintendent for Cambridge Public Schools in Massachusetts and for New London public schools in Connecticut. When I interviewed her, she was serving as the executive director of the Richard Green Institute for Teaching and Learning. She was recruited there for her strong background in mathematics and curriculum development.

Also, by that time she had earned her Masters of Mathematics Education and Doctor of Education from Wayne State University.

Nordmoe hopes to impact the higher education community as she has done for so long in the K–12 school community and now works as a professor at Sacred Heart University. In addition, she is a board member of the American Association of University Women, a founding member of the Minnesota chapter of Black Women in Higher Education, and a former member of the board of directors of Danbury Hospital.

Like the many other women I interviewed for this book, Nordmoe has received many awards throughout her career. They include the Women of Distinction Award from the Mayor of Danbury, the City of Detroit Mayor's Award for Community Service, the Inspiration Women's Award from the Business and Professional Women's Association, and a Resolution from the board of directors of the Danbury Hospital for Efforts to Improve Health Care in the Community.

If she could start over, Nordmoe would stay in the education field. "However, I would pursue positions in higher education. I made a tremendous sacrifice moving around so much," she said.

Nordmoe is divorced with one adult daughter.

Deagelia Pena—"Failure Was Not an Option"
President, Pena Education Center

Deagelia (Dely) Pena is making sure that students in her native country, the Philippines, get a good foundation in the basics early. As president of her own company, she ensures that some of the most needy students there have a chance to flourish. Part of her determination may spring from her own early childhood experiences. Pena told me that in elementary school she performed poorly, so her teachers then probably would not have dreamed that she would grow up and earn four college degrees. She earned a bachelors degree in Education from St. Theresa's College and a master's degree in statistics from the University of the Philippines in 1961. In the United States, she earned another masters degree in mathematics in 1964 and a Ph.D. in Educational Research in 1969 from the University of Michigan.Pena grew up in a small town, Malabon, Rizal (which is now a part of metro Manila). She told me she knew she was well off growing up because her family lived in a big house. "I was neatly dressed and wore shoes while my classmates did not. They wore wooden shoes," she said, adding that the main mode of transportation was horse and buggy and mini buses. Pena's father was an assistant treasurer of their municipality. She had two brothers and two sisters. She does not remember much about her mother because she died when she was only six years old and in the first grade. She does remember that her mother played with her sometimes.

Reflecting back on her elementary school days she recalled, "The reason I was doing so poorly in school was because I skipped classes to go to the new dairy shop to eat ice cream with my classmates." She credits her grandmother with getting her back on track. "At first no one was really looking after my schooling. I practically failed elementary school, but my grandmother was able to talk with my teachers about my work," she said. Consequently, Pena learned the importance of parental involvement in school affairs at an early age.

Pena said her high school years were much better, where she enrolled in a public high school in the Philippines and took an entrance exam. "I found out later that the test was really an IQ test. It placed me in the top section of my class," she said. "I was wondering how this happened since my earlier grades were so low," noting that her previous grades did not match her performance on the test.

With renewed confidence, Pena said she developed a love for math. She continued her high school years at a private Catholic high school, earning high grades. One of her high school teachers urged her to compete for a Fulbright grant, and her success in obtaining that prestigious grant brought her to the University of Michigan. Although Pena did well in college, she said she did not enjoy her college years socially, as she was among some very wealthy students who had private chauffeurs. Even so, "many of the students came to me for help before class," she said.

After moving on and completing her graduate degrees, Pena held several research positions. She started out working with the Appalachia Educational Laboratory as a research and evaluation specialist for one year, and then worked for three years as a research specialist with the Detroit Board of Education. She spent the next three years as an assistant professor in the School of Medicine and as an associate graduate faculty in the College of Education at Wayne State University. Her next career move was to return to her alma mater as associate director for Research in the Affirmative Action Office for three years. After leaving that position, she came to Washington, D.C. to work as a statistical specialist at the National Education Association.

Reflecting on her career, Pena said, " I experienced a lot of discrimination working in the United States. However, I struggled to accomplish a lot by publishing articles and research papers, which no amount of discrimination can stop," she declared. Indeed, Pena has presented papers at the American Education Research Association, American Psychological Association, and the American Statistical Association. She has published almost 50 articles involving research in higher education, interaction analysis, sampling, and other topics.

Aside from receiving the Fulbright Scholarship, Pena has received a number of other honors throughout her career, including being recognized in the *International Who's Who in Education* and in Recognition for First Place on a civil service examination for statisticians.

Pena's community activities revolved around her love for the educational field. She was a former trustee at Gibson School for the Gifted in Michigan, volunteered as a science fair judge for the Washington Statistical Society, and served as a member of the Superintendent's Advisory Committee on Minority Student Achievement in Fairfax County, Virginia.

Pena's ability to remain productive and obtain increasing levels of responsibilities throughout her career has been extremely important to her. It shows that despite the perceived discrimination that she encountered in the United States, she was still showcasing her skills through her latest venture, running a school in her native land.

WOMEN TO WATCH

The last three women that are profiled appear under the label Women to Watch. I hope that by using this label, you will see that there is still plenty of room for the untold stories of more minority women who are making great strides in their careers everyday. I believe that you will hear even more about these three women in the years to come

Beatrice Muglia—"Found the Right Mentor"
Medical Doctor

Beatrice Muglia remembers wanting to be a medical doctor since she was in grade school, and she continued to be deeply interested in the sciences as a teenager. Her problem was she was not sure what she needed to do get there. When she told her guidance counselor that she wanted to study medicine, she was told to study medical technology. That was probably because her SAT scores at the time were low. Fortunately, she found a mentor who brought out her love for math, and her grades in math began to soar. She also began taking optional courses like trigonometry and physics, and these factors set the stage for her to gain admission to college.

Muglia grew up the daughter of a mother who was a homemaker and seamstress and a father who was a railroad machine operator. She had two sisters and one brother. She recalls enjoying her childhood. She participated in science fairs, tutored younger students, and volunteered at her school library. Her high school mentors encouraged her to go on to college.

She took her mentors' advice to attend college and vowed that she would go on to become a medical doctor despite having been discouraged earlier by her high school counselor. She graduated with a degree in biology from the University of Michigan. While there, she said her social adjustment was difficult. "As a Hispanic female, I felt like it was a completely different environment. It was a cultural shock for me," she recalled. "I was really lucky to have a strong mentor to help me stay focused."

Muglia, along with Zina Pierre, was among the youngest women I interviewed. She completed her medical degree in 1992 and followed that with her internship at Henry Ford Hospital in Detroit and her residency at William Beaumont Hospital in Royal Oak, Michigan.

One of her most significant honors and awards at the time was winning a fellowship to Case Western Reserve University Hospital System in Cleveland from July 1997 to July 1998, an experience she said she enjoyed.

Muglia warned that women choosing the medical field should understand that men tend to have more support than women. "Women had to swim on their own in a very male-oriented environment," she said about her experience.

Muglia has given presentations at a variety of medical associations, including the American Gastroenterologic Association, the Clinical Cytomery Society, and related professional associations. She had the opportunity to give a presentation with several colleagues at a National Symposium of Hematology in Targu Mures, Romania.

Muglia is licensed to practice in the state of Michigan, Ohio, and West Virginia. When asked if she would choose the same line of professional work, she told me "Yes, especially now that I have finished everything." Beginning her career as a staff pathologist in Wheeling, West Virginia, she said her salary was already in the $150,000 to $199,999 range. Muglia has proven that she could handle all of the rigors associated with entering a male-dominated career field and "swim on her own" with the right support system as she put it.

Rondalyn Kane—"Unstoppable"
Former Deputy Director of the Women's Bureau

Rondalyn Kane equates her childhood with one of the most popular television shows capturing black family life in the 1980s—*The Cosby Show*. Each of the episodes focused on the typical experience of Bill Cosby and his wife Clare (played by Phylicia Rashad) raising their children, complete with all the challenges of the teen years. The big difference was that unlike many of the roles relegated to black men and women on television, Clare was a high-profile lawyer while husband Bill was a medical doctor.

When I spoke with Kane during her days as deputy director of the Women's Bureau within the U.S. Department of Labor, she fondly recalled her "Bill Cosby family life." She said she grew up in Baltimore, and at the time of the interview, her parents had been married for 43 years. Her mother was a federal government executive, and her father was a senior vice president of a savings and loan company. She had one other sibling, a brother, and she remembers growing up in a Jewish area of Baltimore and going to Jewish schools from the fourth through eleventh grades. "I experienced some prejudice in school, but I was not stopped by it," she said. "I had a great childhood. My parents were loving and supportive. I was told that nothing can stop me from achieving."

According to Kane, her college years at the University of Maryland were a lot of fun. "I was involved in a lot of activities," she said. She told me she was active in a black theater group and active in the community. Even with all of that, she graduated summa cum laude.

Like Jane Smith, Kane originally wanted to be a lawyer. "Around 10, I watched a lot of stories about the civil rights movement on television. I wanted to touch lives and make a difference. I wanted to be a part of Martin Luther King's movement even then," she recalled. However, her career took a more eclectic path. After graduating with a bachelor's degree in political science, she took a position working on Capitol Hill as an associate staff member with the U.S. House Rules Committee in the U.S. House of Representatives. She worked there for seven years. The expectations there were very high. "The Congressman expected only the best. I felt like I had to be a perfectionist," she said.

Kane believes that those experiences on Capitol Hill equipped her for her next position as the executive director of the Congressional Black Caucus Foundation. She stayed in that job for three years, from 1990 to 1993, which by her account was the longest tenure for any other executive director holding the position. Kane was only about 31 years old when she took on that enormous responsibility, and she said that the executive director position equipped her with superior management skills and allowed her to be quite creative with the resource management, especially with little money. She beamed as she said, "One of the major highlights of my time there was putting together the Congressional Black Caucus Weekend. More than 30,000 people came to town [D.C.] for four days." The Congressional Black Caucus Legislative Weekend is considered to be one of the foundation's signature annual events, which includes dozens of workshops, seminars, and town hall meetings and features prominent national leaders in politics, academia, and businesses. In addition, Hollywood entertainers usually make appearances throughout the weekend. After spearheading that effort, Kane told me, "I learned to be unstoppable."

In her next position, Kane spent about a year as a lobbyist for the Service Employees International Union before going to the federal government as a political appointee. When Bill Clinton became President, Kane secured appointments first in the U.S. Department of Health and Human Services and later as deputy director of the Women's Bureau. She stayed in those positions for five years.

Political appointees serve at the pleasure of the president of the United States, and the position can last for days, months, years, or throughout the president's complete term. It is very unlikely, however, that an appointee will serve for a full eight years even if the president is reelected because these positions are highly sought after by campaign workers, donors to the campaign, and various interest groups who may favor certain individuals. Moreover, candidates recommended by congressional leaders, senate leaders, or other elected officials will likely be vying for those same positions as well. In other words, presidential appointments are not easy to acquire, and a candidate needs considerable support to succeed as Kane, Pierre, and Smith did in obtaining one.

The business field was another area of interest to Kane. "I did have my own business for a short time," she told me. "But I had problems with my partner in business so we dissolved it."

Now, Kane is the director of innovation and strategy at National Cooperative Band, Capital Impact, a national nonprofit organization committed to eradicating poverty through innovative community development, lending, technical assistance, and public policy development. Kane's career path shows that she is not only multitalented but is preparing to equip the next generation of leaders with some of the tools that they will need to be successful.

Jocelyn "Joy" Bramble—"Telling Positive Stories" Newspaper Publisher

One of Joy Bramble's worst career memories did not come from her business experiences as a publisher of four local newspapers in Maryland. Rather, it had to do with a grocery store she and her husband bought.

Born in 1946, Bramble grew up in the Caribbean island of Montserrat. Her father owned a store and sold gasoline and coal. Her mother owned a dress shop. With three other sisters, she recalled having a very happy childhood. She married an Anglican Episcopal priest in 1972 after graduating from Queens University in Ontario, Canada, and earning a teaching certificate from the University of Calgary in Canada. Both moved to St. John's Antigua, where her husband worked for St. John's Anglican Cathedral and Bramble worked as a teacher at All Saints Secondary School.

Bramble came to the United States with her husband as he pursued further study at Yale University and continued her work as a teacher for several years. She decided to leave teaching because she did not like it, and instead she decided to join the world of business ownership, like her parents.

Bramble's first business venture was as a store owner. She told me that one of the stores in her Baltimore neighborhood was owned by a Korean. The community where she was living was mostly African American, and she remembered telling her husband that she would buy the next grocery store that was for sale. She soon received her wish as a grocery store became available for $10,000. "The lady wanted $5,000 down. She would stock the store and we could pay her monthly," Bramble said.

The hours were long, and some days she worked from 6 am until midnight. Unfortunately, break-ins were also a problem. "One time," she recalled, "the burglars broke a hole in the bricks. They stole 25 cases of Pepsi, smeared ice cream on the floor, and broke up all the cigarettes in their cartons." She and her husband were shocked and horrified to learn, "someone had even defecated on the floor." "After all we had done for some in the community, this was devastating," she said, adding that they had often given people items on credit and in some cases were not repaid.

As bad as her experience in business was, Bramble never gave up her interest in being her own boss. She took on her next venture—newspaper publishing. The business started in Bramble's kitchen, and she watched it grow from her kitchen table to more than 200,000 readers in Baltimore, Prince George's County, Annapolis, and the eastern shore. The paper emphasizes "positive stories about positive people." Her aim was to challenge the often negative portrayal of African Americans in the media.

Bramble's community service includes working with the University of Maryland School of Medicine Board of Trustees, the Maryland Education Coalition, and the Goodwill Industries. She holds annual health-care screenings, women's forums, literary events, and other events sponsored by her foundation, the Times Community Services, Inc. She was a founding member of the Montserrat Historical Trust, the first museum on her native island.

Bramble is listed in *Who's Who Among Women Businesspersons,* which is quite appropriate given her penchant for actively pursuing other business ventures. She works as a founding partner with a design and technology company and a Maryland-based mortgage company, too.

Now that you know more about the career choices of the 14 women that I interviewed and the heights that they obtained in their chosen career field, the chapter to follow will reveal each woman's own definition of success. Is it financial? Is it achieving a goal? Or is it something else?

NOTES

1. Susan Horsburg et al., "Rags to Riches," *People,* August 2004.
2. Ibid. and see Charisse Jones, "Owning the Airwaves," *Essence,* October 1998.
3. Horsburgh et al., "Rags to Riches."
4. Johnnie Roberts, "The Power of One," *Essence,* October 2007.
5. Lynn Norment, "Cathy Hughes: Ms. Radio," *Ebony,* May 2000.
6. Roberts, "The Power of One."
7. Norment, "Cathy Hughes: Ms. Radio."
8. Ibid.
9. Jones, "Owning the Airways," 112.
10. Standard & Poor's Stock Report, Radio One Inc., March 2008.
11. Ibid.
12. Ibid.
13. Black Entertainment Television, "Debra Lee Succeeds BET's Bob Johnson," news release, June 2, 2005.
14. Rashaun Hall, "Talkin' BET with Debra Lee," *Billboard,* October 2005.
15. R. Thomas Umstead, "BET's Revival Mission: Debra Lee Tries to Shake Off the Network's Bad Rap," Multichannel News, October 2007.
16. Patricia Sellers, "The Women of Viacom," *Fortune,* October 2006.
17. Abe Lubetkin, "Success Is about Risk-Taking," *The Brown Daily Herald,* February 2007.
18. Ibid.
19. David Goetzl, "A Decent BET," *Broadcasting and Cable,* September 2007.
20. See Dudley Products, Dun & Bradstreet, http://www.selectory.com.
21. John Maynard, "Firmly Anchored," *The Washington Post,* July 30, 2006.

22. S. A. Reid, "Big Footsteps, Sharp Focus, Bold Mission: Jane Smith Succeeds Dorothy I. Height as Leader of Black Women's Council," *Atlanta Journal*, February 5, 1998.

23. Ibid.

24. Mosaica Education, "Mosaica Education Names Dr. Iris Metts as Chief Education Officer," news release, February 27, 2003.

Chapter 4

FACTORS RESPONSIBLE FOR CAREER SUCCESS

What makes the 14 women portrayed in this book successful? You may be surprised to learn that the answers they gave are not much different from some of those uncovered in Chapter 2, which discussed the various theories (i.e., social capital, human capital) that could be used to explain career success. That chapter described a large number of social and psychological factors that were believed to contribute to the career success of both minority and white women. For example, we found that obtaining a terminal degree (Ph.D.) was an important factor in obtaining career success for those interested in senior academic positions.

In addition, we found from Gene Landrum's work that some individual traits like passion, drive, confidence, and competitiveness were important psychological traits of the successful blacks that he studied. In addition, we found that among administrators in public schools who rated themselves as "very successful," being active in professional organizations was of great career value, a common concept explored in social network theories. Some of these studies suggested also that those who attended a special-focus institution (i.e., a minority or women's college or university) were more likely to obtain career success than their counterparts in coeducation institutions. Let us now see which, if any, of these social or psychological factors were thought to be the most salient factors in explaining the career success of the 14 women that I interviewed.

Rather than provide a checklist, I allowed each woman to tell me the first success factor that came to mind. The advantage of this approach is that I would not get back information in which they would likely rate all items highly. I wanted them to focus on themselves and not on what they thought I might want to hear. That approach helps me tell their stories free of interviewer bias, which can occur when categories are suggested to respondents. Consequently, I recorded their first response to the question, "What factors do you consider most responsible for your career success?" After that, I recorded any second or third responses that the women gave.

Table 4.1 shows their answers at a glance. Although all of the women had a first-choice answer, some did not have a second or third choice.

As you can see from Table 4.1, the factor that was considered most important to the women's career success was their own drive. Webster's dictionary defines drive in various ways, but three of those definitions give an idea of what these women had in mind. First, drive can be considered "an organized effort to accomplish a purpose." Next, it is also a strong motivating tendency or instinct that prompts activity toward a particular end." Finally, Webster's dictionary states that it can be synonymous with the terms "initiative, energy, or aggressiveness." Taken together, the definitions essentially suggest you should be doing all that you can to get ahead. You may find yourself in many situations where your decision, and your decision alone, can affect the outcome of how you advance on the job. That may include such situations as deciding whether to join various professional associations, deciding how involved you will be in these organizations once you join, deciding whether to take additional job training or classes,

Table 4.1
Most Important Factor in the Women's Career Success

1st Choice	2nd Choice	3rd Choice
Personal Drive: **43%**	*Family:* **38%**	*Mentors/Others:* **40%**
Cathy Hughes	Cathy Hughes	Eunice Dudley
Dely Pena	Iris Metts	Dely Pena
Iris Metts	Gail Nordmoe	Bea Muglia
Debra Lee	Dely Pena	Rachel Petty
Gail Nordmoe	Bea Muglia	
Bea Muglia		
Family: **36%**	*Networking:* **23%**	*Networking:* **20%**
Jane Smith	Zina Pierre	Andrea Roane
Rachel Petty	Jane Smith	Debra Lee
Joy Bramble	Gwen Baker	
Eunice Dudley		
Andrea Roane		
Religion: **14%**	*Education:* **15%**	*Religion:* **30%**
Rondalyn Kane	Rachel Petty	Jane Smith
Zina Pierre	Debra Lee	Cathy Hughes
		Gail Nordmoe
	Personal Drive: **8%**	*Personal Drive:* **10%**
	Rondalyn Kane	Gwen Baker
Mentors/Others: **7%**	*Confidence:* **8%**	
Gwen Baker	Eunice Dudley	
	Religion: **8%**	
	Andrea Roane	
Total 100%	**Total 100%**	**Total 100%**
(n=14)	(n=13)	(n=10)

*(Totals may not add to 100% due to rounding.

deciding whether to pursue high-visibility assignments, deciding when to apply for advancement opportunities, deciding when to move on to another company or business, and/or deciding when to fight for your rights when workplace violations affect you.

To further clarify this notion of using your own drive for career success, let us look at a few hypothetical scenarios in which personal drive could come into play. I will then discuss some of the comments that the six women made on the issue of personal drive.

SCENARIO ONE

You have been hired for an entry-level position with a company. Your boss asks you and another coworker to take a short course that will increase your understanding of the next project that will be assigned to you and the coworker. The supervisor says it is not mandatory but it will probably be helpful. Which of the following choices would you make? You decide (a) Maybe your coworker will take the course and you can get the information from her/him, (b) You already have a college degree and you don't know why you need to take another class, or (c) You tell your supervisor that you appreciate being asked to take the course and then gather all the information that you need to register for the class.

Your best strategy for success here would be to take your supervisor up on his offer and register for the class. Why? It shows that you are motivated to do your best on your next project. You want to do all that you can to improve your knowledge base on the job when given the opportunity to do so. Your supervisor could have told only your coworker about the class, thereby depriving you of the opportunity. Now, if you thought you should pass on this opportunity and let your coworker take the class, it is likely that your supervisor will not see you as someone who wants do more than sit back. Whether this is a true impression or not, you may run the risk of this negative perception, which could affect later opportunities. Next, if you hold yourself back by thinking you have done enough simply because you have your college degree, such an attitude can convey a lack of drive since you are not taking advantage of potential opportunities as they come your way. Your supervisor may not debate that it is a good thing that you had the drive to obtain that college degree, but as radio executive Cathy Hughes said, "A college degree does not assure success." While Hughes told me education was important, it was not in her top-three choices. I think she realized how so much of her success was an incredible struggle against the odds. Recall that she had a baby as a teenager and did not complete her college degree. Nevertheless, she achieved incredible success in the radio industry that even resulted in her receiving several honorary doctorate degrees.

Going back to the hypothetical example above, you may not be blessed to have a supervisor like the one described. Instead, you may have supervisors who resent you having more education than they do or who do not appreciate educational credentials. They may have made it to their position as part of the old boy's network or some other means unrelated to actual job qualifications. If this is the case, you will have to use your drive to get a new position with a more supportive supervisor.

SCENARIO TWO

Supposed you are a seasoned worker now. You have received some promotions that recognize your achievement in the company already. Yet, you have not been able to reach the highest staff level or management position in your company. From your own assessment, you don't think you will be moving up anytime soon and you perceive you are not on the fast track like some of your coworkers. You could (a) Forget about getting any more promotions and just continue doing your job until you retire, (b) Let your supervisor and others know that you are ready to move up to the next level and start applying for relevant job openings both within your department and outside of it, or (c) Let your coworkers and others throughout the organization know that you feel you are stuck and are not happy about it.

In this hypothetical scenario, answer (b) would be the best choice for demonstrating your drive to move ahead in your career. In this case, you are actively applying for new jobs that match your qualifications. You are not waiting for your supervisor to tap you on the shoulder and say what a great job you are doing or how hard you are working and yet still not deliver a promotion to you. You are taking those matters that you can control into your hands. Although applying for new positions does not mean that you will receive a promotion, it will go a long way in demonstrating that you are taking the initiative to accomplish your goal of receiving your next promotion.

MINORITY WOMEN TALK ABOUT PERSONAL DRIVE

Now, recall from Table 4.1 that Cathy Hughes, Debra Lee, Iris Metts, Beatrice (Bea) Muglia, Gail Nordmoe, and Deagelia (Dely) Pena named their own drive as the main ingredient in their career success. Let's see what some of their comments revealed on this factor.

Dely Pena told me, "My own drive led to my interest in learning. That was the most important factor that led to my career success." One example of Pena's drive for career success came when she seemed to be stuck at a "rank five" professional level instead of the highest, rank six. She filed a lawsuit, which eventually resulted in her position being reclassified to the higher rank six. Although she did not get the next management position that she wanted, she was able to retire and thereby increase her compensation by thousands of dollars. At the time of the interview, Pena said she earned more than $90,000.

An example of millionaire business executive Cathy Hughes's drive is illustrated in her almost single-minded pursuit of owning a successful radio company. Although she started with little money and ended up sleeping in her building when she was able to buy a radio station with her son, she did not give up in her attempts to obtain the financing needed to make her radio business a success. Hughes was willing to perform the most menial tasks of her business along with the management duties to keep it going—even in the face of possible foreclosure at one time. Hughes said, "I absolutely loved radio. Anything that you love is easier to do." Not only was it easier to do, but her drive made it worth all the hardships that she went through before making it big in the industry.

Former Prince George's County School Superintendent Iris Metts told me, "My own determination was most responsible for my success. I remember setting specific goals years ago. I knew I wanted to go to college and work in the educational field." She added, "When I first started thinking about obtaining a doctorate, I knew where it could take me." Indeed, Metts did go on to complete her doctorate in education. She started teaching, moved up to a principal position, then an assistant superintendent position, and later a superintendent position after a stint with the governor of Delaware. Her work with the governor was a major breakthrough for her, too, since she was appointed to his cabinet as the secretary of education. As superintendent of the Prince George's County public school, Metts told me that she earned between $200,000 and $249,000.

Black Entertainment Television (BET) CEO Debra Lee indicated, "I was motivated to work hard." Although Lee's career change from a law firm (she was a Harvard Law School graduate) to BET surprised many around her, she believes that her hard work fueled her dedication to helping the company become more successful. Lee told me, "I had no real mentors. The people around me provided guidance." The founder of BET, Robert Johnson, was one of the people around her who hired her. Johnson, too, was a savvy businessman who was determined to make his company a financial success. With Lee's help, his wife, and the other management team and staff, Johnson sold the company to Viacom for $3 billion, making most of his top executives rich in the process. Even before the company was sold, Lee told me she earned over $500,000.

Gail Nordmoe, an educator, told me about one example of her drive to excel while she was an elementary public school teacher in the Detroit public school system. After teaching for about three years, she remembered asking to teach some of the lowest-achieving students in the district. According to Nordmoe, the students were mostly poor African Americans, Southern whites, and Hispanics. Nordmoe was troubled by the lack of understanding students had with mathematics. As a specialized math teacher she had the option of asking for another placement in schools in need of mathematics teachers. "When I went to the personnel office I told them I would like very much to teach math, preferably in a low-income community," she said. "The personnel administrator asked me, 'Are you aware of what you are asking?' I told her I wanted to help those children. She gave me three schools to visit and told me I could select one. I picked one located where the Detroit riots had occurred."

Nordmoe was not surprised that the students were in a dysfunctional school and that they were not well disciplined. In addition, because of where the school was located, they were used to having a substitute teacher for an entire school year. "On my first day at this school, the students threw their books out of the window. I talked with them about that. I told them we needed those books to share with other students," she said. "I had to establish a routine with them with clearly defined rules and expectations. They finally realized that I would be coming back and they began to have good feelings about me." Nordmoe had high expectations for the students, and it paid off.

When invited to speak at the Michigan Council of Teachers of Math at the University of Michigan, Nordmoe took her students with her. "I wanted to demonstrate how inquiry-based learning could be used in mathematics for low-achieving students. I had been trained to use discovery, an inquiry-based approach to teaching mathematics by some of the leading mathematicians of that period, such as Robert B. Davis and Zolton Dienes," she said. Later the assistant superintendent for that region recognized her success with these students by appointing her to be a demonstration teacher for the entire region. "That position set me on a path to training other teachers using these methods. The work of these children really put me on this path," Nordmoe explained. Indeed, her drive to do more for low-achieving students helped her move on to higher-level positions. Nordmoe described it this way: "The reinforcement that these children gave me by succeeding encouraged me to apply for other positions that could impact more students and teachers." These positions included being an assistant superintendent of schools in Danbury, Connecticut, and Cambridge, Massachusetts.

Finally, medical doctor Bea Muglia believes that she had a tremendous amount of discipline. "I was motivated to stick to my goals and not let anything or anybody stop me from becoming a doctor," she said, adding that it was important for her to do well in school even though her parents could not help her much, as her mother was a seamstress and housewife and her dad was a rail-road machine operator. "I was interested in the sciences and participated in the science fairs," she said. With the help of a mentor, Muglia was able to attend and graduate from the University of Michigan. From there, she went on to Michigan State Medical School. At the time of the interview, Muglia told me she was earning between $150,000 and $199,999.

As the stories of these five women show, it is clear that they see individual action as the main determinant in their career success. As will be discussed later, they feel a combination of other factors also helped them achieve career success.

MINORITY WOMEN TALK ABOUT FAMILY SUPPORT

The next five women said family support was the most important factor responsible for their career success. Whether it was a father, mother, aunt, uncle, or another close family member, they believed family members either individually or jointly set the framework for getting them interested in the career choices that they made. Former CEO Jane Smith, business owner Eunice Dudley, news anchor Andrea Roane, newspaper owner Joy Bramble, and educator Rachel Petty rated the family as their first choice. Following is a sample of how they saw the family as playing the most crucial role in their career success.

Rachel Petty said she had a very supportive and nurturing family, stating that "my parents created a lot of opportunities for me." One example that she recalled was being able to work for an uncle who owned a bank. "I worked there every summer from the 10th grade and on through college. I really liked working with numbers," said Petty. Her parents were responsible for her getting hired. This type of family influence shielded her from facing the rejections that many youth who lack connections experience before landing a professional position.

Jane Smith, former CEO of Business and Professional Women/USA, said her family upbringing was most responsible for her later career success. "My father was the first black dentist in Atlanta. My mother was a public school teacher," Smith said. "My grandmother was the first black superintendent of an all-black school system. She had an office in City Hall." Jane recalled, too, that her grandmother was a student of famed scholar and Harvard University graduate W. E. B. Du Bois. Aside from this, Jane said her grandmother started a Girl Scout chapter in her area and indicated that she belonged to Jack and Jill, a cultural and social group in which mostly middle-class students were invited to join. Smith credits many of these early experiences with paving the way for some of the other opportunities that she was offered later in life. Her access to family members in key workplace positions show that this allowed her to network early in life and put her in a position to learn about various workplace positions that may be of interest to her. For example, she held her first professional job while she was in high school when she traveled to Harvard University to work on a Project on Girls in the University's School of Education. "I really like the professional side of the work. I loved my colleagues and supervisors. They were very brilliant and quick," she said. Such early exposure undoubtedly made a big impression, and Smith later graduated from Harvard University with a doctorate in education and social policy.

Millionaire business owner Eunice Dudley strongly believes that having a good family upbringing contributed to her career success. Her father was a minister and her mom was a teacher. Born in the deep South, Dudley was the seventh of nine children. She does not believe that she thought much about being successful back then, however. "It evolved for me," she said, adding that her aunt and uncle were responsible for getting Dudley her first professional job as a Fuller products salesperson. They were already in the business. With her family's support she worked in door-to-door sales in New York, where she met her husband, Joe, who also worked for Fuller. They soon married and she left college while Joe continued in the business. Since times were hard, she took a job as a legal secretary to help support her new family. "We reinvested the money Joe made back into the business," she said. Their years of struggle eventually paid off as they acquired mentors (another couple in the business) to advise them on other key aspects of growing the business. Obtaining mentors was Dudley's third factor for success, and having confidence (a psychological trait) was considered as second in importance for her success.

Another interesting point that Dudley made was that even before becoming successful in the cosmetic business that she and her husband run jointly, her experience working at this law firm had a positive influence on her. "It was very professional," she said. "It was located in a building of other black professionals. There was North Carolina Mutual Life Insurance, an architecture firm, Covington and Associates accounting firm, Sampson Pharmacies, and five or six doctors' offices. I didn't come in contact with other races. There were a lot of professionals in the building and I had a chance to see them operate and emulate them." It seems that her parent's middle-class status afforded her the opportunity to be exposed to these varied professionals, which had quite an impact on young Eunice.

News anchor Andrea Roane, like the other women mentioned so far, told me, "My parents pushed me to obtain the best education wherever I found myself." Here you see the combination of factors highlighting both the parental role and the emphasis on education as major factors in Roane's success. Not surprisingly, her mother was an elementary school teacher and her father was a railroad station manager. She and her family could travel for free. "I remember going to Paris with my grandmother. It was an eye-opening experience. It really opens your mind when you travel," she said, adding that there is a great deal of education in travel, too.

Roane remembers always wanting to be on the honor roll. "My mother demanded excellence," she said. Before becoming a television anchor, Roane was a teacher. Growing up, she pretended that she was a teacher with her dolls. With a facility for foreign languages, Roane said she could have worked at the United Nations or the State Department. However, after moving from her teaching position, one of the big breaks that came in her career was moving on to television. After hosting a McNeil-Lehrer newscast, she had numerous job offers that "snowballed into my work at NBC." The effect of history, a concept, described by Bell and Nkomo in an earlier chapter on views about success, can be gleaned from Roane's next remark about this barrage of good fortune in the job market. "I came along during an era when employers were looking for people of color and women. I did not have a struggle story, I just worked hard at what I did," she said. At the time of the interview, Roane said she earned between $300,000 and $499,999.

Joy Bramble, newspaper owner, rounded out the group of women who saw family as the most salient factor in their career success. "My mother had a shop making hats, but my father was the major breadwinner," she recalled. Her father owned a store selling gasoline and coal. "The money my dad made allowed us (she and her four sisters) to have extra things." Bramble remembers her dad "always telling us that we were special. We knew we were expected to go to college," she added.

Before getting into the newspaper business, Bramble was a teacher, and she followed that experience to become a grocery store owner. She opened her first small business that consisted of two neighborhood grocery stores in West Baltimore. Bramble believes that seeing the hard work of her dad and mom definitely stayed with her and ultimately allowed her to fulfill her own business dreams.

The examples above are just a sampling of the ways that each of the women believed that their families started them on their path toward successful careers. Although you cannot choose the family that you are born into, it is important to realize from these stories that there are numerous ways that the family serves as an agent of socialization, one that exposes you to various experiences, contacts, and financial resources that, when used properly, can lead to career success. Even if you are raised by a single parent or don't receive the kind of support that these women described, you can always reach out to an aunt, uncle, or some other family member who might be able to provide jobs or job leads. Also, in some cases reaching out to another adult could prove beneficial, whether it is a teacher or someone who wants to serve as a mentor.

WHAT ELSE IS IMPORTANT?

Table 4.1 shows that the remaining women that I interviewed thought religion, other adults/mentors, or education was the most important factor in their career success. The role of other adults/mentors has clearly emerged in some of the other women's stories and does not need to be expanded upon here since they perform some of the same functions and roles as a family member would in many instances.

With respect to religion, however, Zina Pierre's comment is typical of how religion plays a role in the women's career success. On this factor, Pierre said, "Having a relationship with God helps to balance the adversities I deal with in the workplace." Indeed, religion appeared as the second or third choice for some of the other women that I interviewed.

Since we constantly hear about the link between education and earnings from Census Bureau's data and elsewhere, you may ask why more of the 14 women did not include this key factor in their first-choice listings. Although I did not ask the others why education was not in their first choice, I suspect that because all of the women were exposed to and/or graduated from a college or university, some with multiple degrees, that this was seen as a given and not worth mentioning. Table 4.2 clearly indicates that the women I interviewed are among the highly educated. Six women held doctorate degrees as their highest degree, and five others held an M.A., J.D. or M.D. Only two of the women (Cathy Hughes and Eunice Dudley) did not complete their college studies, but due to their tremendous achievements in business were later awarded honorary doctorate degrees from some of the nation's most prestigious universities, as shown in Table 4.2. Also, remember that two other women, Rachel Petty and Debra Lee, did mention education as their second choices for their career success.

Turning back to Table 4.1, the most frequently cited second choice for the women was the family, followed by networking, a key concept of social capital theory. Zina Pierre said, "It is important to be in the presence of other strong women who demand excellence in everything that you do." Minority women can find these contacts by joining such organizations as the National Council of Negro Women, the National Congress of Black Women, and the Business and Professional Women's Association. For Pierre, the National Council of Negro Women played an important role in supporting her appointment to a top position

Table 4.2
Educational Background of Successful Minority Women

Woman	Highest Degree	College/University
Cathy Hughes	High School, Honorary Ph.Ds	Attended Creighton University and University of Nebraska
Debra Lee	J.D.	Harvard University
Eunice Dudley	High School, Honorary Ph.D	Attended North Carolina A&T State
Andrea Roane	M.A.	University of New Orleans
Iris Metts	Ed.D.	Virginia Polytechnic and State
Zina Pierre	M.A.	Howard University
Jane Smith	Ed.D.	Harvard University
Dely Pena	Ph.D.	University of Michigan
Gail Nordmoe	Ed.D.	Wayne State University
Gwendolyn Baker	Ph.D.	University of Michigan
Rachel Petty	Ph.D.	University of Maryland
Beatrice Muglia	M.D.	Michigan State University
Rondalyn Kane	M.P.A.	University of Southern California
Joy Bramble	B.A.	University of Calgary

in President Bill Clinton's administration. Not only was she a member of this group, but also she had strong ties to some of the top leaders of that organization.

Table 4.1 shows that mentoring, networking, and religion (all key concepts in social explanations for explaining career success) were among the third responses that some of the women gave in explaining their career success. On mentoring, one of the women in this category added, "The kind of support I received from adults in my environment (not my parents but from relatives and professionals like teachers and ministers) was important. People saw ability in me." The remarks made about networking and religion did not differ much from those women previously mentioning these concepts.

Across all three of the choices that most women mentioned, we can clearly see the interaction of both psychological factors (personal drive) and social factors (supportive family members, networks) in explaining the career success these women have enjoyed.

CONTRIBUTION OF OTHERS TO THE SUCCESS OF MINORITY WOMEN

Another way to explore how the women viewed their role in relation to others as contributing to their career success was to ask several follow-up questions. I asked each of the women to give me a rough estimate of the contributions that they believed others made to their success. The women were asked, If you can attribute your success to somebody in achieving your position today, what was the contribution in terms of a percentage? The women could select from self, mother, father, teacher, mentor, employer, or someone else. They were asked to assign percentages that totaled up to 100 percent.

Generally, the women attributed as much as 20 percent to 30 percent to mentors, employers, parents, spouses, or networking associations. Some respondents, however, gave sizable contributions (50 percent or more) to their mothers (Nordmoe, 75 percent), or themselves (Pena, 50 percent; Lee, 60 percent; and Bramble, 50 percent). Muglia gave a 70 percent contribution rating to her mentor, while Dudley gave a 50 percent contribution rating to her mentor. Muglia explained her choice of giving 70 percent to her mentor this way, "Sometimes the success you achieve depends on the environment you are in. My parents were not able to help me so much financially or academically, but my mentor was able to do this. The ratio that you attribute to someone can change depending on your parents' background."

MINORITY WOMEN'S AWARENESS OF BEING SUCCESSFUL

The majority of the women (10 of the 14) that I interviewed said they were aware of their desire to be successful since they were very young, as early as grade school. A couple said they were aware of their desire in high school (Metts) or after college (Pena). The remaining respondents said they didn't really think about success much (Dudley, Hughes). Dudley said, as mentioned earlier, "Success evolved for me." The comments by those who believed they were aware of their success very early often involved them having visions of holding a leadership position, teaching other kids, or imagining that they would be very rich. Pierre said, "As a kid I had this attitude that I could do anything I wanted to do. I wrote a lot of poetry at seven and I was very popular." Smith said, "I remember my mom would make us kids take naps. I had visions of leading and speaking and being in charge like my grandma."

Although no single factor emerged as the sole explanation for the women's career success, the joint contribution of social factors—family members, mentors, religion, and psychological factors (individual drive or determination) emerged as playing an important part of their career success. Since about equal proportions of our respondents attended a women's university or college versus a coeducational university, I cannot say that attending a special-focus college or university was more significant than not doing so. In addition, most of the respondents seem aware of their desire to be successful at an early age. This is important since it suggests that children should be continuously exposed to a variety of career opportunities through family, professional, and school networks.

Also, interviewing a representative sample of minority women would have been extremely useful. That would help us test whether factors associated with particular theories, such as human capital theory (educational levels, drive/effort) or social capital theory (involvement in networks etc), continue to be important in the career success of a broader group of minority women.

None of the women mentioned any organizational features of their workplace that were important to career success in their three top choices. However, you will see that this is not the case when the women are questioned about the obstacles that they encountered in their road to career success. They have a lot to say about features of their workplace then.

Contrary to a lot of discussion in the popular literature, almost none of the minority women thought that their minority status aided them in their career. Thus, being Hispanic, Filipino, or black was not helpful for most of the women I interviewed. Only Andrea Roane believed that she came along during a time when employers were looking to hire people of color and women. As you will learn, most saw their race and gender as major obstacles in their climb to the top. Details on these obstacles and others will be explored in the next chapter.

Chapter 5

OBSTACLES TO MINORITY WOMEN'S CAREER SUCCESS AND WHAT TO DO ABOUT THEM

WOMEN IN THE LABOR FORCE

Recent reports show women, and minority women in particular, to be underrepresented at the highest levels of government and private-sector organizations. For example, a 2006 Women in the Labor Force Databook report showed that about 59 percent of women were in the labor force. Minority women, especially black and Hispanic women (10 percent and 8 percent, respectively), are less likely to be represented in management, business, and financial operations occupations than white women (14 percent, as shown in Table 5.1). Black and Hispanic men are similarly underrepresented in this occupational category. Higher concentrations of Hispanic and black women (about 30 percent) find themselves working in service occupations compared to white and Asian women (less than 20 percent). Similarly, the earlier President's Interagency Council on Women report found that "women are seriously underrepresented in all levels of government, elective office and as candidates for political parties." Another major study, by the Federal Glass Ceiling Commission, showed that a glass ceiling exists, and it operates to exclude minorities and women from the very top levels of management in the private sector. White males fill most of the top management positions in these corporations. What accounts for these disparities by race and gender?

The Glass Ceiling Commission's comprehensive work revealed a range of problems that account for the underrepresentation of women in general and minority women in particular in obtaining career leadership positions. The Commission found that the barriers to advancement of minorities and women exist on three levels: societal, governmental, and internal. The problems identified more than a decade ago are relevant today.

SOCIETAL BARRIERS

The Commission identified two major societal barriers that perpetuate a glass ceiling for minorities and women: the supply barrier (opportunity

Table 5.1

Women and Men Employed in Management Occupations

	Black	White	Asian	Hispanic or Latino Ethnicity
Women				
Management, Business & Financial (%)	10.0	13.8	14.5	8.3
Total all occupations (Thousands)	8,410	53,950	3,011	7,725
Men				
Management, Business & Financial (%)	9.7	16.7	16.9	7.1
Total all occupations (Thousands)	7,354	64,883	3,511	11,867

Note: Corresponding percentages of women in service occupations were Hispanic (31 percent), Black (27 percent), White (19 percent) and Asian (18 percent)

and achievement) and the difference barrier (stereotypes, prejudice, and bias).

Regarding the supply barrier, the Commission noted that large numbers of minorities and women are nowhere near the "front door to Corporate America." Members of minority groups tend to be disproportionately represented among the working poor. In other words, they tend to be overrepresented in low-wage occupations, in part-time work, and in seasonal jobs in the informal and secondary economies. They also suffer high unemployment.

The other societal obstacle, the difference barrier, describes how minorities and women have to contend with attitudes that stem from widespread acceptance of stereotypes. The Commission suggested, "If the only Hispanics or Asians and Pacific Islanders individuals one ever meets are waiters and parking lot attendants, the tendency is to believe they all are like that." Additionally, the Commission's New York public hearing pointed out that the exploits of African-American, Asian, or Latino gang members or drug users are regularly reported in the media. These social encounters and portrayals reinforce how the general public views all members of these communities. Such stereotypes can then form the beliefs upon which people act.

Ann Morrison, an expert on women's issues, argued that, "Of all the barriers to corporate advancement identified, it is prejudice that tops the list, or the prejudgment that someone who is 'different,' such as a female executive, is less able to do the job."[1] She found that the major differences that lead to discomfort are cultural, gender, and color-based differences.

GOVERNMENTAL BARRIERS

The Commission further identified three governmental barriers to the advancement of women and minorities. They were lack of vigorous and consistent monitoring and law enforcement, weaknesses in the collection and disaggregation of employment-related data, which make it hard to determine the status of groups at the managerial levels, and inadequate reporting and dissemination of information relevant to glass-ceiling issues.

INTERNAL BARRIERS

Finally, the internal barriers that exist inside corporations were related to the view that many middle and upper-level white male managers view the inclusion of minorities and women in management as a direct threat to their own chances for advancement. One illustrative comment shared at a Commission hearing is telling: "If they are in, there's less of a chance for me. Why would I want a bigger pool? White men can only lose in this game. I'm endangered."

Given this attitude voiced by some, it is not surprising that the Commission found a host of internal barriers related to inadequate outreach and recruitment, the existence of a climate in the organization that fosters different communication styles and ideas of what is appropriate and acceptable behavior in organizations, and corporate pipeline barriers that block the access of an individual to the top. According to the Commission, if the CEO at the top does not demand accountability, then minorities and women are often subjected to policies and practices that act as barriers to their advancement. These pipeline barriers that affect opportunities for advancement include:

- Lack of mentoring
- Lack of management training
- Lack of opportunities for career advancement
- Lack of opportunities for training tailored to the individual
- Lack of rotation to line positions or job assignments that are revenue producing
- Little or no access to critical developmental assignments, including service in highly visible task forces and committees
- Different standards for performance evaluation
- Little or no access to informal networks of communication
- Counterproductive behavior and harassment by colleagues
- Initial placement and clustering in relatively dead-end jobs or highly technical professional jobs

The Commission indicated that, "In any given setting these practices are tailored to different groups in different ways, but the end result is the same—they all strengthen the glass ceiling." That is why it is important for women to recognize these practices early in their career.

Let us examine more closely one of the practices—harassment—mentioned by the Commission. Several of the women interviewed for this book could remember various instances of harassment that they or someone else they knew encountered on their way to the top. According to Mary Sawyer's report on harassment, the English word "harass" derives from a French word meaning "to set the dogs on."[2] In contemporary use, she explains, it means "to trouble, worry, or torment, as with cares, debts, repeated questions, etc." Although the Commission mentioned harassment by colleagues, an even greater threat to minority women's career success is racial harassment by a supervisor.

AN ILLUSTRATION: THE HARASSMENT CASE OF ROBIN W.

A sample case study of one minority female professional captures a full range of harassment tactics that might occur in today's workplace. The case of Robin W. vividly portrays the racial harassment that she experienced from her white supervisor. Robin was a black female employed by a large association in Washington, D.C. The 12 harassment tactics that follow show some subtle and not-so-subtle behavior designed to derail Robin's career advancement:

1. Asked to Apply for Work in Another Division

Robin's supervisor told her to apply for a job vacancy in another unit. Her white supervisor indicated that there were no promotion prospects for her in the unit where she worked. The supervisor gave her the vacancy notice with a smirk.

2. Assignment to Work Projects That Are Already Behind Schedule

Robin was asked to take over a major national project from another male colleague that was behind schedule. Once she received the assignment, numerous attempts were made to sabotage the project through losing portions of the project work, rushed time lines, refusal to allow peer review of the work, refusal by some managers to discuss written comments they had made, and not providing the final corrections to Robin for review prior to publication of her report.

Another example of this form of harassment experienced by Robin was being given an assignment to prepare an hour-long presentation for a "black" conference on short notice. No mention was made that the manager knew the request had been made earlier for another staff member who did not want to give the presentation. An added insult occurred when her white supervisor told her that a "black" should make the presentation.

3. Engaging in Fishing Expeditions for Complaints About Work

Robin's supervisor tried to create dissatisfaction with her work among customers. On one occasion, her supervisor contacted Robin's client and wanted to know if the client was unhappy with the way things were going on the project. The client told the supervisor that everything was going smoothly. The client informed Robin of this strange encounter with her supervisor after that conversation.

4. Receiving Anonymous Threats

Robin received an anonymous letter, which contained a large black spot in her workplace mailbox one morning. Robin interpreted the large black spot as threatening. The black spot has some analogies in grade school literature and was synonymous with a death threat (see the "Black Spot" chapter in Robert Louis Stevenson's *Treasure Island*).

5. Assigning Unnecessary Work

Robin's supervisor neglected to inform her that the preparation of a summary from a lengthy project was not necessary. Although Robin's client informed her supervisor that the summary was not needed, her supervisor never conveyed this information to Robin. She let Robin stay late to continue working on the unnecessary summary.

6. Instituting Petty Work Requirements

Robin's supervisor changed record-keeping formats three or four times. She then singled out Robin to say that the information that she received on several of Robin's projects were on obsolete forms. None of Robin's other colleagues or the unit secretary knew what forms the supervisor was requesting.

7. Creating Negative Relations With Other Colleagues

Attempts were made to isolate Robin from her other colleagues. On one occasion, her supervisor announced that some workplace files were missing. Her supervisor asked a support staffer if any of the missing files were in Robin's office. In this instance, the supervisor was implying to the support staff that Robin was the problem. On another occasion, Robin's supervisor would have her secretary write notes to Robin to document some "error" in Robin's timekeeping. Here, the supervisor was trying to develop a paper trail that she could use against Robin later.

8. Assigning Last-Minute, Manufactured Rush Assignments

Robin's supervisors tried to hurt her performance by giving her last-minute, manufactured rush projects with inadequate preparation time. For example, she was given an assignment to develop a survey with a three-day time limit. She was told to attend a work group meeting without information about the time of the meeting or where the meeting was located. She was told to "check around" and find out that information. Additionally, Robin was asked to review an anonymous research paper. When Robin raised questions about the purpose, author, date of the paper, and the author's name and affiliation, her supervisor cancelled the assignment.

9. Negative Remarks in Performance Appraisal

Robin's supervisor began placing unjustified negative remarks in her performance appraisal. This practice began after Robin complained about not being promoted to the next grade level.

10. Shouting at Employees

Robin's supervisor shouted at her for not attending a staff meeting. This shouting was done even though Robin's supervisor knew that she had a meeting already scheduled with another higher-level agency official. All of this was done so that several other staff members heard the commotion. One apologized to Robin for the supervisor's unprofessional behavior.

11. Threats of Insubordination

Robin's supervisor threatened her with charges of insubordination for not attending a staff meeting. She followed up her verbal threats with a written memo saying that if Robin missed another staff meeting without supervisory approval to do so, appropriate action would be taken against her in the future. Robin did not miss the staff meeting, but she was able to attend only part of it since she had previously scheduled a meeting with high-level agency officials.

12. Over-Scrutiny of Use of Leaves

While on leave due to the death of her father, Robin received calls from her supervisor asking many of the same questions that she had already discussed with another supervisor. In addition, the supervisor sent Robin letters requesting that she return to work by a certain date. Upon Robin's return, her supervisor would not meet with her to discuss the "urgent" work that she needed to perform until days later. Another incident involving Robin's leave occurred with the death of her grandfather. Robin was denied her entitled bereavement leave when her grandfather died during the same time period that her brother-in-law died. Robin had to file a grievance with the union to get her leave restored. The organization granted leave benefits for each bereavement period.

The above examples of the tactics used by some supervisors represent just the tip of the iceberg. They all require a thoughtful and careful response in order to reduce career setbacks. In Robin's case, it is clear that all of these tactics were undertaken to create a hostile and uncomfortable work atmosphere for Robin. Indeed, given the large volume of harassment tactics directed at Robin, it is likely that the supervisor's intention was to derail Robin's career advancement and/or force her out of the organization eventually. Robin decided to sue and left the organization after one year to start her own business.

If you experience harassment similar to Robin's, you must decide whether to sue, file a complaint with the organization, or find another job. If you decide to sue, you should be prepared for a costly and lengthy legal process. You have to find an excellent attorney (who cannot guarantee that you will win your case). Remember, you will get a chance at justice, as you will discover later from the stories Dely Pena shares. Also, you will attend many meetings with your attorney, respond to many interrogatories about the facts of your case, and participate in depositions answering questions from your agency's lawyers.

At the same time, you must continue to actively document the harassment incidents for your records, even if you decide to find a new job as soon as possible. It is important that you locate a support group like 9to5, the National Association of Working Women, too. That organization has a national hotline and can respond to your questions about whether your case might be considered by an attorney because your employer has violated Title VII of the 1964 Civil Rights Act. (That Act prohibits discrimination in employment on the basis of race, sex, color, national origin, and religion.) Also, passage of the 1991 Civil Rights Act allowed, for the first time, compensatory and punitive damages to the victims of illegal employment discrimination. 9to5 can put you in touch with other women who have experienced similar instances of harassment who will share their stories with you about how they responded, which can be very helpful as you decide what is best for you.

OBSTACLES IDENTIFIED BY OUR WOMEN ACHIEVERS

Some of the 14 women interviewed readily recalled other multiple barriers that affected their career advancement. Using the same framework as the Glass Ceiling Commission, the women identified the societal barriers (supply or difference barrier), governmental barriers, and/or internal barriers within the organizations where they worked.

Five of the 14 women achievers mentioned what the Commission called the difference barrier of gender, race/ethnicity, or age as major obstacles that they encountered in their workplaces. The women recalled instances where they believed one or more of these characteristics negatively affected their workplace experiences. Decision makers (i.e., supervisors) and/or colleagues saw these women as different and judged them in a negative light based on prejudice, stereotypes, or other biases.

Typical of the remarks regarding gender bias was that of educator Dr. Rachel Petty: "The main obstacle to my success has been the questioning of whether a woman or a minority could do the job. I have found that in some workplaces there is a little club where some believe that men should be in power. That goes for the racial issue, too. You have to find your own support."

Dr. Deagelia Pena, a Filipina, pointed to her ethnicity as a problem for her. "My ethnicity has been the most significant obstacle to reaching my career goals. I've been in a nonsupportive environment where there is suppression and blocking in my quest to achieve something, even just trying to fulfill the duties of my job," said Dr. Pena, who added that she found this particular organizational culture to be "racist, hypocritical, and anti-intellectual."

INTERNAL BARRIERS WITHIN THE ORGANIZATION

The women of this study gave examples of five of the pipeline barriers that affect opportunities for career advancement identified in the Commission report. Among those was the harassment experience by colleagues. The five pipeline barriers mentioned by our women achievers were lack of mentoring, initial placement in highly technical professional jobs, lack of opportunities for training tailored to the individual, lack of access to critical development assignments, including service in highly visible task forces and committees, and balancing career and family.

1. Lack of Mentoring

Business executive Debra Lee said that she was unable to find a law partner who would help fight for her success when she worked for a law firm. She decided to leave that law firm to pursue other career options at Black Entertainment Television (BET).

2. Initial Placement in Highly Technical Professional Jobs

Educator Deagelia Pena believed that she was hired at one level below the highest staff level (at that time a rank 12) despite being more qualified than anyone else in her branch at the time. Pena revealed that this made it hard for her to move up to the top staff job or move into another area as a manager. She said managers viewed her as a skilled statistician.

3. Lack of Opportunities for Training Tailored to the Individual

One of the women who asked that her identity on this topic remains anonymous reported that she experienced problems due specifically to other employees who clashed with her leadership style. If she had received more training, she said she may have been able to help her subordinates understand and accept the way she wanted things done. Those employees who were not used to being held accountable by previous supervisors saw her rather than their own shortcomings as the problem in getting the job done.

4. Little Access to Critical Development Assignments, Including Serving on Highly Visible Task Forces

Deagelia Pena believes that another major obstacle to her career success was the exclusion from some key developmental assignments, including serving on highly visible task forces and committees. She recalled one incident in which the president of the organization wanted her to work on a highly visible project. Her supervisor refused to let her do the job requested directly by the president.

5. Balancing Career and Family

The last example of internal pipeline barriers experienced by several of the women related to the familiar problem confronting women in general, including minority women. Former school superintendent Dr. Iris Metts said balancing career and family was another major obstacle that she confronted. "There is this feeling of wanting to do it all. I don't think this one is any different from young white women striving for career success," she said.

GOVERNMENTAL BARRIERS

Educator Pena was the only top achiever of the 14 interviewed who described one of the governmental barriers that affected her career advancement. Pena said she filed a lawsuit as a way to achieve access to a promotion within the organization. The earlier Commission study, for example, found that there is a lack of vigorous and consistent monitoring and law enforcement of EEO laws that would ensure the inclusion of women and minorities at higher levels in the organization. Pena said the organization vigorously fought the lawsuit, which went all the way to the Supreme Court. According to Pena, her case was a real miscarriage of justice, and the organization was allowed to get away with discriminatory treatment toward its minority women employed in her division. "Sometimes justice does not prevail," she said. "Young minority women should be especially mindful of this when they file a legal complaint."

OTHER SIGNIFICANT OBSTACLES FOR BUSINESS OWNERS

Two other women described problems related to business growth. Business executives Cathy Hughes and Eunice Dudley cited the familiar problems of obtaining financing for their businesses. Seeking funds to get a business off of the ground has long been a problem for startup businesses.

NO MAJOR OBSTACLES IDENTIFIED

Surprisingly, two top achievers believed that success came easily. Television anchor Andrea Roane said, "I came along during an era when employers were looking for people of color and women. I just worked hard at what I did. I remember hosting the McNeil-Lehrer newscast. When I finished that show, people started offering me jobs and interviews. This snowballed into my current position in Washington, D.C." Similarly, Zina Pierre, an assistant to former President Bill Clinton, said, "I believed success came pretty easily because I was willing to learn new things and work hard." It is likely that Roane's visibility on this show and Pierre's political contacts, along with hard work, helped to shield them from some of the obstacles described by the other women. This is most evident in Pierre's remarks about some of the obstacles likely to affect young minority women, discussed in the next section.

GREATEST OBSTACLES THAT WILL AFFECT YOUNG MINORITY WOMEN

When asked about the greatest obstacles that will affect young minority women today, the women interviewed for this book said that some of the problems they encountered will still be relevant to their younger counterparts. Even more of the women pointed to continued barriers related to race and gender. The number of women who felt this way exceeded those who admitted experiencing a race and/or gender barrier themselves. For example, 10 of the 14 top women achievers in this book pointed to what the Commission called societal or internal barriers (gender, race, balancing career and family, and lack of opportunity) as the greatest obstacles that will continue to affect the careers of young minority women. Following are some examples illustrative of what these top achievers had to say:

- "Access is a big problem. Young professionals don't have the kinds of contacts and influence they need to get to the next level. People don't realize how important that is to obtaining your position. I had the unique opportunity of having people like Alexis Herman, Dr. Dorothy Height, and Dr. C. Delores Tucker help me. That is the kind of help

that some people can only dream about."—Zina Pierre, former special assistant (to President Bill Clinton)
- "Being a woman, first, a lack of mentors and career opportunities, second, and race, third."—Dr. Jane Smith, nonprofit executive
- "Opportunity to move up in the profession. There are so few opportunities in a field of your interest. A college degree does not assure it."—Cathy Hughes, business executive

Although networking and access are important, Dr. Deagelia Pena cautions that minority women should not naively believe that members of their own race or ethnicity would automatically be inclined to help them. "Remember, those up in high places are not necessarily willing to help you. You still have to watch your back with people who are your color." Pena, an educator, cautioned young women to watch out for other minorities who are in positions of power by sharing this experience: "I recall one of my former managers, a black man, intentionally equating my accent as a communication problem. He included this in one of my evaluations. I asked him point blank whether he meant that my having an accent meant that I had a communication problem. His response was that, 'this is an Anglo-centered society.' He did this to hurt my chances for promotion. In fact, I did not get that promotion and ended up filing a lawsuit."

Another high-level woman interviewed for this book who did not want to be identified shared an experience that dampened her interest in trying to help minority women "I recall hiring a younger black woman and ended up fighting her (administratively) after I had to let her go. At the time, I thought she would be an excellent worker. But she did not have all the skills that she needed to be in charge of a staff. She was so concerned about office politics and dressing well. There was a lot of disarray at this agency. So I had to implement change. That experience put a damper on me assuming that you can reach out and help women," she said.

Dr. Beatrice Muglia contends that being in the right location is critical to a young woman's career success. For example, Muglia explains, "The environment that they grow up in can be a big obstacle. It is important to be in the right environment where you can find the support that you need to help you excel." In this instance, she was talking about problems associated with women staying in communities that are too isolated.

Taken together, these remarks point to those social factors that young minority women should continue to weigh in their workplace goals. They can then design effective strategies to cope with these possible career obstacles. Having done this, they may be able to avoid painful setbacks to their career advancement. The women interviewed for this book clearly see these barriers as continuing for future generations of young minority women.

TIPS TO OVERCOME SOME CAREER OBSTACLES

Given that some obstacles identified by the Glass Ceiling Commission more than 10 years ago are still mentioned by the highly successful women interviewed for this book, an important question to ask is what tools can minority women use to avoid career pitfalls? However, before discussing the advice given by the 14 women achievers, it is crucial that minority women think about the totality of the obstacles even these highly successful women encountered. By doing this, minority women may think more carefully about where they are seeking employment. For example, it can be gleaned from the women interviewed that young minority women should ask at least six questions when making a career selection.

QUESTIONS TO ASK FIRST

1. How many women occupy positions of supervisory authority in this organization?
2. How many minority women occupy positions of supervisory authority in this organization?
3. What types of positions do minority women hold in the organization?
4. How long do minority women remain in their position before being promoted?
5. What types of complaints/lawsuits have been filed against the organization?
6. What are the educational backgrounds of those in supervisory positions?

The answer to the first question gives you an idea about how women are treated in that organization. That is, are company policies working effectively to help women move into positions of authority? Get the company's annual report and see what differences exist between men and women holding supervisory positions in the organization. Even if you see that you are entering an organization where few women are in supervisory positions, you are entering that organization fully aware that gender bias may be a possible problem in that organization.

Next, find out as much as you can about the number of minority women who occupy positions of supervisory authority in the organization. Knowing the actual number of minority women gives minority women valuable information about the diversity of the organization. Clearly, if few minority women hold positions of power in a prospective place of employment, moving up in that particular organization could take quite a bit of time—maybe longer than your original career plans. Indeed, the Glass Ceiling Commission study found that the best predictor of promotion rate for black women was time. In their estimation, "If you wait long enough you will be eventually promoted." Joining a company with few minority women holding positions of supervisory authority is a warning sign that you will have to be more vigilant in seeking out other mentors and sponsors to facilitate your career advancement. Also, you should not assume that in organizations with few minorities that those few will be willing to help you just because you are a minority woman. To do so may be a costly mistake, as Dr. Pena revealed earlier.

If you are seeking employment at a primarily minority organization, the question of how many minority women hold positions of supervisory authority is still relevant. Although racism may not be a factor there, there is still the possibility of gender discrimination, which should be examined. That is, how are women advancing in relationship to their male colleagues?

Regarding the question of what type of positions minority women hold in the organization, it is helpful to know if minority women have access to a full range of employment options within that organization. If your review reveals that minority women are mostly concentrated in lower-paid positions, recognize early that advancement opportunities may be limited in that organization.

In ascertaining how long minority women remain in their position before being promoted, you should carefully obtain as much information as you can from various sources—formal and informal—to see if minority women as a group tend to stay in their positions longer than other groups before being promoted. Use this information to assess whether you think racial bias is at work here or some other reason before deciding whether you want to join this organization.

The question about lawsuits and complaints will perhaps provide you with some detailed information on how an organization treats it employees as well. Since few organizations are likely to include data on their internal problems, it is imperative that minority women check with their networks to uncover this type of information about perspective employers. You can contact the Equal Employment Opportunity Commission to learn of major cases that they are pursuing. Remember, Dr. Deagelia Pena pointed out that initiating a lawsuit could be a lengthy process that often hurts the employee. You will need a great deal of stamina and finances to pursue a legal option. For example, read the case of *Roberts vs. Texaco (A True Story of Race and Corporate America)* for a detailed account of Bari-Ellen Roberts' discrimination case, the destruction of evidence by her employers, the use of racial epithets captured on tape, and ultimately her multimillion-dollar settlement.[3]

Finally, determining the educational backgrounds of those in supervisory positions provide some clues about how much the organization values education for their employees. If you find that few supervisors hold higher education credentials than you do, think very hard about joining this organization if you aspire to top-level positions. Dr. Pena, for example, said that prior to her lawsuit she was assigned to work for a woman who had been promoted to management with a high school diploma as her only educational credential. "The woman was one of management's favorites," said Dr. Pena.

> Do not let the stereotypes and prejudices of others hold you back from what you want to achieve.

Now that you know some of the questions to ask before seeking employment in a perspective organization, the next section offers tips that the women achievers believe will help you on your way to the top. These tips, while not meant to be exhaustive, will encourage you to think more deeply about the challenges that you will likely confront in the workplace.

ADDRESSING THE DIFFERENCE BARRIERS

Race: The Difference Barrier

Tip: Plan ways to meet your goals. Don't let people or circumstances define what you can be. Dr. Rachel Petty, an educator, reminds young minority women to stay focused on the big picture. You should not let the stereotypes and prejudices of others hold you back from what you want to achieve. Indeed, many of the minority women interviewed recognized that young minority women have to adopt a variety of coping mechanisms to deal with instances of racism or discrimination that they may encounter when they enter the workforce. According to some of the women interviewed, women could discuss the problem with the person or persons responsible for the racist or discriminatory acts, file an internal grievance, file a complaint with the Equal Employment Opportunity Commission (EEOC), hire a private attorney, or plan to leave the organization if the situation arises to such an unpleasant level that it is adversely affecting their health.

Dr. Pena warns that filing a complaint through agency channels or even outside channels will likely make the situation far worse for the woman since the agency will typically use a large amount of its resources to defend itself against the charges. Also, employers will not necessarily tell the truth that they are sworn to tell in court. Unfortunately, some agency officials have no problems engaging in dishonest tactics, including lying under oath, coercing other workers to lie under oath, and shredding and/or forging documents.

Gender: The Difference Barrier

Tip: Although there are ceilings to achievement in some work places, don't go around with a chip on your shoulder because you are a woman. This advice, from Dr. Iris Metts, applies to white women too.

> Women should not allow themselves to become so absorbed with problems related to gender that they take on such negative attitudes that their colleagues find them unpleasant to be around.

> Find good mentors in your neighborhood, professional associations, and/or religious institution.

Like the race barrier mentioned previously, problems related to gender may also arise in the workplace. Some of the women interviewed indicated that the men in supervisory authority over them questioned whether a woman could do the job.

The message emphasized in Metts's advice is that women should not allow themselves to become so absorbed with their problems related to their gender that they take on such negative attitudes that colleagues find them very unpleasant to be around. As mentioned for the race barrier, minority women will have to decide if the treatment that they receive in the workplace rises to the level of gender discrimination. If so, the minority women and/or other women must determine for themselves if the best course of action is through informal or formal complaint channels.

ADDRESSING VARIOUS INTERNAL ORGANIZATION BARRIERS

Lack of Mentors

Tip: Find good mentors in your neighborhood, professional association, and/or church. Zina Pierre, former special assistant to U.S. President Clinton, urges young minority women not to wait for your workplace to institute a mentoring program if one does not exist. Young minority women must be vigilant in identifying potential mentors regardless of their race, ethnicity, or gender who have expressed an interest in their career advancement. Typically, if you attend a church or other religious institution, there are a number of auxiliary groups—whether charitable, governance, or other—seeking active participants. As a result of your work there, you can meet others who may have advice and contacts that may prove useful either at the current time or at a later date.

Some of the professional women's organizations that seek to empower women of color include The National Congress of Black Women, founded by the late Shirley Chisholm and followed by the dynamic leadership of the late Dr. C. DeLores Tucker. One of the most important tasks that Dr. Tucker undertook on behalf of minority women was forming a Commission for the Presidential Appointment of African American Women. Her leadership in this area was responsible in part for recommending hundreds of qualified minority women to serve in both President Clinton's administration and later President Bush's administration. Although some of the women had some contacts already supporting their appointments, there were many others that came to the White House's attention primarily because of the stature and endorsement of Dr. C. DeLores Tucker.

> Don't stay in a mediocre work environment where your skills and abilities are not appreciated.

According to some of the women interviewed, other organizations that minority women may find helpful to their careers include the National Council of Negro Women, founded by Dr. Dorothy Height. As Zina Pierre pointed out, "Minority women need to get involved in women and family organizations because they link you to resources, people, jobs, leadership training, and workforce development."

Dealing With Access to Critical Development Assignments

Tip: Take responsibility for obtaining greater access to assignments by expanding your horizons and meeting new acquaintances in and outside of your workplace. Dr. Pena offered this tip because it took her a long time before she realized how important being proactive in the workplace is in your quest to move up the career ladder. Developmental assignments can prove crucial in preparing the employee to succeed in even more visible and complex assignments. The contacts you make may be able to recommend you for other developmental assignments that could be beneficial in your workplace or pave the way for new, more challenging positions elsewhere. It is important to note that the key is to assess your situation and determine whether you are indeed receiving some developmental assignments or none at all. Prior to promotions, supervisors often provide opportunities for selected employees to work on projects that allow them to gain increased responsibilities.

An even more ambitious approach regarding failure to receive critical developmental assignments comes from Dr. Gail Nordmoe: "Don't stay in a mediocre work environment where your skills are not appreciated. It drains your energy." She gave this tip based on her many years of experience in academic environments. Dr. Nordmoe believes that you will do much better to move on to another job if your supervisor is not assisting you in your career development. That means keeping your resume up to date and staying informed of current job opportunities as well.

Dealing with Lack of Opportunity for Training

Tip: Make sure you get a good education. Not surprisingly, most of the women achievers interviewed stressed the importance of education towards

> It is important for women and others to be lifelong learners.

> ## Try to work with others who want to work hard.

career advancement. These women repeatedly said that minority women, like all other women, need to work hard in school and get a good education. This point was emphasized even more for minority women because of the dual biases of race and gender stereotyping that some of them experienced in the workplace. The earlier Glass Ceiling Commission found that equal educational preparation for white and African-American women did not yield similar advancement opportunities for African-American women. More white women than African-American women were in the top management levels of their companies. Nevertheless, our achievers believed that once minority women are armed with the best education they can obtain, they will feel more confident in the workplace decisions they make. That includes seeking out educational trainings that they may have to pay for themselves. Businesswoman Cathy Hughes added this tip: "It is important for women and others to be lifelong learners. Learn from your mistakes." Although Hughes did not complete a formal degree, she said she was always taking courses to help her career. Her hard work and extra course work eventually led to her phenomenal business success. Even with all the honorary doctorates that she has received, she definitely recommends that minority women still complete their academic degrees.

ADDRESSING YOUR OWN MOTIVATIONS

Dealing with Lack of Motivation

Tip: Finally, almost all of the women interviewed emphasized the drive that minority women must constantly maintain in order to succeed in their workplaces. You must actively take responsibility for trying to advance in your workplace. In other words, you should be motivated to work hard and not wait for someone else to praise or recognize you before you are willing to work hard on tasks assigned by your supervisor. As TV anchor Andrea Roane pointed out, "Some young women don't realize how hard they still have to work. Doors will not open automatically just because you are young, good looking, or graduated from a good school. You can't go from a college degree to an anchor position overnight."

Several other women offered suggestions for maintaining one's drive to work hard. Nonprofit executive Dr. Jane Smith suggested this tip: "Try to work with others who want to work hard. They will inspire you further and vice versa. You still have to produce results." In other words, when you know that some coworkers are slackers, don't volunteer to work on teams with them. It can create the impression that you do not want to work hard either.

Similarly, medical doctor Bea Muglia offered this tip related to the drive to work hard: "Maintain as much discipline as you can. Don't dwell on office politics that involve romantic entanglements or rumors." The concern that Dr. Muglia raises involves the tendency by some people to waste valuable work time discussing office dating relationships or speculating about office favorites or office enemies. All of these things may surface in your workplace at some point. Nevertheless, you need to have enough discipline to continue on with your work while being mindful of how such relationships might impact your performance and possibilities of advancement.

If, on the other hand, you find that romantic relationships between coworkers or supervisors or unwanted romantic attention directed toward you impact your ability to do your job, it is your responsibility to identify agency resources and outside sources to resolve these problems. Don't wait for someone in the agency to rescue you. The problem of sexual harassment can surface in your workplace as discussed in Chapter 2. Regardless of the obstacles that minority women encounter in the workplace, the drive to find a solution is a major component of their ability to achieve success in their chosen career field.

You Can Overcome Obstacles

Clearly, the identification of some of the obstacles to career success for minority women in this chapter represent an initial step. It is hoped that by drawing advice from the collective comments of the 14 prominent women interviewed for this book, other minority women will feel compelled to share more detailed stories on how they coped with various workplace barriers. By doing so, future generations of young minority women will be equipped with the tools that they need to overcome the myriad workplace problems they may confront.

The advice from the women interviewed for this book can go a long way to help minority women take advantage of all that their workplace offers, too. Women can tailor this advice to their own individual circumstances. The 14 women who candidly shared their stories provide only a glimpse of the extraordinary career success these women were able to achieve in spite of the difference, governmental, and internal barriers that they faced.

Notes

1. Ann Morrison, *The New Leaders: Guidelines on Leadership Diversity in America* (San Francisco: Jossey-Bass), 1992.

2. Mary Sawyer, *The Harassment of Black Elected Officials: Ten Years Later* (Washington, D.C.: Voter Education and Registration Action Inc., 1989).

3. Bari-Ellen Roberts and Jack White, *Roberts vs Texaco: A True Story of Race and Corporate America* (New York: Avon, 1999).

Chapter 6

LOOKING AHEAD: SOME CAREER FIELDS THAT NEED MORE MINORITY WOMEN

N ow that you know more about some of the career interests of the 14 minority women interviewed, you may be interested to learn more about the professions these women chose. Recall that the women I interviewed included physicians, business owners, chief executive officers, educational administrators, and top government officials. Regardless of your career choices, I would like to emphasize some of the professions needing more women, especially minority women. Many more choices are listed in various *Occupational Outlook Handbooks,* produced by the U.S. Department of Labor, and the *Encyclopedia of Careers and Vocational Guides.*[1] Both books provide details on the nature of the work, educational requirements, earnings, and suggestions for additional resources. With that in mind, let us start with the medical field since it is an area with few minorities, whether male or female.

THE MEDICAL FIELD

A recent report by the Association of American Medical Colleges reveals that there is still a need to increase the pool of racial and ethnic minority physicians.[2] In 2004, African Americans, Hispanics/Latinos, and Native Americans comprised only 6.4 percent of all physicians graduating from medical schools in the United States.[3] Additionally, the percentage for Asians was 5.7 percent. For the most part, the percentage of men far exceeded the percentage of women in each of these racial and ethnic groups. The gap between men and women was smallest between African-American men and women. Even though the number of minorities has increased over the past 20 years, the small numbers show that there would be considerable opportunities for those willing to invest in the lengthy college preparation, residency, internship, and testing required to obtain a medical doctor's license. Typically, it requires a four-year undergraduate degree, four years of medical school, and three to eight years of residency or internship based on the field selected.[4] Medical doctor Beatrice Muglia, as you may recall, emphasized the importance of discipline, too. "It is really hard when your friends call and you have to study," she said.

The 2008–2009 *Occupational Outlook Handbook* provides an excellent over-view of the nature of the work, detailed training and other qualifications required, advancement opportunities, and job outlook and earnings for physi-cians and surgeons. Physicians and surgeons are among the highest-paid occupa-tions. Using information from the Medical Group Management Association, the report shows the following median compensation of various types of physicians:[5]

Table 6.1
Median Compensation of Various Physicians

Type	Salary
Anesthesiology	$259,948
Surgery (general)	228,839
Obstetrics/gynecology (general)	203,270

Although these salaries are high, I do want to emphasize that you must first be admitted to medical school. This step is probably something that may be taken for granted by many young people, who are often bombarded with messages from the popular culture indicating that the American dream can be achieved with hard work only. Also, if you were able to gain admission to the undergradu-ate college of your dreams, it may seem that you did so with remarkable ease. On the other hand, if you kept your high school grades up, had great recommenda-tions, wrote a really good essay, scored quite high on the SAT or ACT, and still did not get into some of the colleges of your choice, you can expect the same when applying to medical school or graduate school. In other words, prepare yourself for even more competition as you seek graduate school admission, as medical school is extremely competitive and you should not become too upset if denied your first-choice school. Just make the effort and prepare to do the best you can on the admission exams, and keep trying until you get into one of the 146 medical schools in the country.[6] Think about the drive and determination of the women portrayed in this book and never give up. According to the women studied here, your family, social support networks, and religious values should help you meet this challenge.

I have met too many young people who feel crushed and defeated when they are not accepted into their dream schools, despite having very high grade point averages (some 4.0) and scoring highly on the SAT exams. That is especially true for those applying to the Ivy League schools like Harvard and Yale, which receive tens of thousands of applications from around the world for a limited number of slots. Keep in mind, too—as some of our women achievers noted—that race and gender did make a difference in their struggles for career success, and it may be a factor also in your quest to gain admission to some of these schools. We have not reached the color-blind society that Martin Luther King Jr. spoke of so eloquently. However, if you prepare yourself mentally now, you will not take the rejections as personally. Just remember that these rejections can be overcome if you persist, as some of the women achievers profiled in this book did. You will have to pick and choose your battles, but you can prevail if you persevere.

POLITICS

According to the U.S. Office of the Clerk data files, 38 women of color have served in Congress. Most (almost 75 percent) were elected since 1990.[7] Clearly, with 435 representatives in the U.S. Congress, there is still a need for more minority women to consider this career option. As Representative Diane Watson said in her comments about this book, "We need you in the House and the Senate too." Shirley Chisholm had the distinction of being elected in 1969 as the first African-American woman, while Patsy Mink served as the first Asian American in 1964, and Ileana Ros-Lehtinen followed in 1989 as the first Hispanic woman. The complete listing from the Office of the Clerk is shown in Table 6.2.

You can see from this listing how long it has taken minority women to obtain representation on the two major political party tickets. African-American women have fared better than their Hispanic and Asian-American counterparts. Even so, most of the African-American women seem to come from a few states, like California and Florida.

Although seeking a congressional or senate seat usually involves seeking a local or state elected office first, some minority women have managed to get themselves elected without doing so. Congresswoman Donna Edwards is a recent example of someone who succeeded in obtaining a Congressional seat by virtue of her community activism and political support from other local elected officials. She defeated a black male incumbent to become the first black woman from Maryland to join the congressional ranks.

Getting started in the political arena is fairly simple. You can volunteer in one of your local politicians' campaigns. There are school board races, county council seats, county executive races, and statewide and national races taking place in your area regularly. Also, members of the U.S. House of Representatives are elected every two years while members of the U.S. Senate are elected every six years. The exact titles of various elected official positions may vary for some of the local or state races, depending on local or state custom or law. You can work for a Democrat, Republican, or Independent, depending on your political interests.

One of the most important benefits of volunteer work in the political area is that it will let you find out early if this is a career that interests you and is a good fit. You will learn whether you like working the unorthodox hours, distributing campaign literature, planning and attending fund-raising activities, and dealing with pleasant and unpleasant members of the public. Political work is not a 9-to-5 job. It may routinely require evening and weekend work and traveling around the city, county, state, or country depending on the office you are seeking.

Table 6.2
Women of Color Who Have Served in the United States Congress

Name	Party/State	Date of Service	Ethnicity
Patsy Mink	D-HI	1965–1977; 1990–2002	Asian-Pacific American
Shirley Chisholm	D-NY	1969–1983	African American
Yvonne Burke	D-CA	1973–1979	African American
Barbara Jordan	D-TX	1973–1979	African American
Cardiss Collins	D-IL	1973–1997	African American
Katie Hall	D-IN	1982–1985	African American
Patricia Saiki	R-HI	1987–1991	Asian-Pacific American
Ileana Ros-Lehtinen	R-FL	1989–present	Hispanic American
Barbara-Rose Collins	D-MI	1991–1997	African American
Eleanor Holmes Norton	D-DC	1991–present	African American
Maxine Waters	D-CA	1991–present	African American
Carol Moseley Braun	D-IL	1993–1999	African American
Corrine Brown	D-FL	1993–present	African American
Eva Clayton	D-NC	1993–2003	African American
Eddie Bernice Johnson	D-TX	1993–present	African American
Cynthia McKinney	D-GA	1993–2003; 2005–2007	African American
Carrie Meek	D-FL	1993–2003	African American
Lucille Roybal-Allard	D-CA	1993–present	Hispanic American
Nydia Velázquez	D-NY	1993–present	Hispanic American
Sheila Jackson Lee	D-TX	1995–present	African American
Juanita Millender-McDonald	D-CA	1995–2007	African American
Julia Carson	D-IN	1997–2007	African American
Donna M. Christensen	D-VI	1997–present	African American
Carolyn Cheeks Kilpatrick	D-MI	1997–present	African American
Barbara Lee	D-CA	1997–present	African American
Loretta Sanchez	D-CA	1997–present	Hispanic American
Stephanie Tubbs Jones	D-OH	1999–2008	African American
Grace Napolitano	D-CA	1999–present	Hispanic American
Hilda Solis	D-CA	2001–present	Hispanic American
Diane Watson	D-CA	2001–present	African American
Denise Majette	D-GA	2003–2005	African American
Linda Sánchez	D-CA	2003–present	Hispanic American
Gwendolynne Moore	D-WI	2005–present	African American
Doris Matsui	D-CA	2005–present	Asian-Pacific American
Yvette Clarke	D-NY	2007–present	African American
Mazie K. Hirono	D-HI	2007–present	Asian-Pacific American
Laura Richardson	D-CA	2007–present	African American
Donna F. Edwards	D-MD	2008–present	African American

You will learn also how the politicians shore up support through grass-roots efforts involving teams of volunteers who typically help get the candidates' message out in public forums, such as mailings and interviews with various print, broadcast, or radio media. All of this grassroots work will acquaint you with a variety of duties associated with campaign work. Not surprisingly, a lot of work and money are often required at the local level, with increasing amounts of both needed as candidates broaden their reach to the state or national level.

If you decide now that running for an office at the local, state, or national (Congressional) level is too much for you, you can always try to make a contribution by working on the staff of an elected official. For example, a recent article in the *Occupational Outlook Quarterly* provides an excellent overview of the various positions available in a legislator's office, including chief of staff, legislative aide, or press secretary.[8] The article also details the pros and cons of working in politics. At the national level, the Congressional Placement Office has a form that you can complete to express interest in various staff positions. Similarly, the Senate Office offers free interviews and a resume bank for those interested in those positions. Obtaining a recommendation from other elected officials that you are close to will likely help you gain the attention of Congressional representatives.

EDUCATION

Although occupations listed in the educational field were not mentioned in Chapter 1 as being in the top-10 highest paying occupations, I want to discuss this area with you because we minorities are not well represented in some key occupations sorely needed in our community. For example, remember that Dr. Iris Metts and Dr. Gail Nordmoe rose to achieve a superintendency position and an assistant superintendency position in their respective fields. Currently, the American Association of School Administrators estimated that, in 2006, women constituted 21.7 percent of those in the superintendency position. That number has increased from their findings in 2000, which showed that only 16 percent of women held that position. The group found that whites (93.9 percent) overwhelming held these positions when compared to the percentage for minorities (6.1 percent).[9] The percentage for individual racial and ethnic groups was much smaller, at 2 percent or less. These numbers demonstrate that there is still considerable room for minority women to ascend to this top level. However, like the medical profession, this position usually requires extensive training beyond high school, as most superintendents hold a doctoral degree. Many had mentors or political supporters who were close to the elected officials or school board members who hire the superintendent. Recall that Superintendent Metts, in addition to her outstanding professional credentials, had ties with the governor of Delaware, who appointed her to lead the Department of Education prior to her move to the Prince George's County School System.

Being responsible for the educational outcomes of an entire public school system is a formidable task. However, it can be extremely rewarding if you want to make a difference in trying to eliminate the disparate test scores currently existing between minority students and other students. Our school systems need the voices, experiences, and leadership of those willing to make tough decisions to improve the lives of our children, and especially our minority children given the disparities in standardized test scores. Remember, you may have to start out as a teacher and rise through the ranks, as some of the women I interviewed did. Please don't think that you will graduate from college and graduate school and move right into these top positions. It took Dr. Metts and Dr. Gail Nordmoe years to rise to a superintendency position. Dr. Nordmoe emphasized the need for more minority women in this field when she told me, "I have been trained in traditional models of leadership, but I believe that there are differences in how women interpret and implement various leadership models. There are elements of compassionate listening, nurturing, and support that a woman introduces into whatever leadership style that she has adopted to assist her along the road to success." She is convinced that gender makes a key difference in succeeding in this field, despite the obstacles that you may encounter.

Along these same lines, minority women are not well represented in the top position of our nation's colleges and universities. At Ivy League institutions, you will hear Brown University President Ruth Simmons mentioned frequently because she is the first African-American woman appointed to lead an Ivy League university. Also, Shirley Jackson is quite well known, having taken on the presidency of Rensselaer Polytechnic Institute. She was also the first black woman to be appointed chair of the Nuclear Regulatory Commission. Minority women, and African-American women in particular, are making more progress in obtaining the presidency of some of our nation's historically black colleges and universities, too.

I spoke with the Ron Blakely, deputy director of the White House Initiative on Historically Black Colleges and Universities, about minority women representation at these institutions.[10] Ron told me that about 20 of the 105 historically black colleges and universities, or 20 percent) are headed by minority women. Blakely believes the numbers are increasing because some of these women have been able to obtain a series of positions, such as department chair, dean, and provost, that helped them obtain sponsors who would support their new role as president. He expects more women to move up into the presidency ranks as the men who held the position for years begin to retire. If you are interested in this top position, you can learn some of what it takes from women like Dr. Rachel Petty, one of the women I interviewed, who has worked in a number of higher-education positions prior to becoming dean at the University of the District of Columbia. Although Petty has not reached the presidency yet, don't be surprised if you hear her name in years to come. The lesson here is that it usually takes a long-term commitment to assume the presidency of a college or university if you are a minority woman. In some unique circumstances, women like Dr. Julianne Malveaux obtained the presidency of Bennett College without having held other roles in higher education. For the most part, however, you should think of that as the exception rather than the rule.

LEGAL FIELD

Another career area greatly in need of more minorities in general, and minority women in particular, is the field of law. According to a 2005 report, *Miles to Go: Progress of Minorities in the Legal Profession,* minority representation in the legal field is "significantly lower than in most professions."[11] The report indicates that minorities represent about 9.7 percent of those in the legal profession. Based on the 2000 Census, that figure compares to 20.8 percent for minorities employed as accountants and auditors, 24.6 percent employed as physicians and surgeons, and 18.2 percent employed as college and university teachers. Examining these figures even closer, you will find that African Americans represent only 3.9 percent of lawyers, followed by Hispanics at 3.3 percent. Another disturbing point made in the report is that the "pace of African-American entry into the profession has slowed in recent years and is significantly slower than that of Hispanics or Asian Americans."[12] Minority women made up 44 percent of the minority lawyers. The report shows further that minority women represent only 1.1 percent of general counsel in the Fortune 1000 companies, a point further underscoring the critical need for more minority women lawyers.

Currently, the proportion of both minority men and women being accepted into law school is quite low. According to the *Miles to Go* report, total minority representation among law students has dropped from 20.6 percent in 2001 to 20.3 percent in 2003 and 2004.[13] The report indicates that most of the drop is due to a drop among African-American law student attendees. Their numbers have fallen from 7.4 percent to 6.6 percent, which represented a 12-year low in 2004.[14] Part of the problem seems to be related to the reliance by law schools on LSAT scores (the legal exam required for all law school entrants).

The *Miles to Go* report makes the point that "most law schools based admissions decisions significantly on students' LSAT scores, despite the fact that this criterion serves as a barrier to minority access."[15] The report indicates further that the LSAT is a weak predictor of law school grades and is not related to professional success as a lawyer. The law school admission process involves other requirements, such as a college grades, personal statement, and references, among other criteria. Some of the most competitive legal programs, such as those in the top-tier schools like Harvard, Yale, or Stanford, show the median LSAT scores of their admitted students to be quite high. Consequently, you should not overlook some of the top historically black law schools, such as those at Howard University and North Carolina Central University. You may find additional support systems in place at these schools that do not sufficiently exist elsewhere for minority students. Even if you want to attend other law schools where mid-level scores are acceptable, the work is still likely to be very rigorous. Here you need to know that graduate school life is another major adjustment. If you are admitted to a law school, you may need to maintain a 2.0 GPA minimum in order to continue in law school. (The exact GPA may vary depending on the law school.) That is a big difference from undergraduate school, where you will still be allowed to stay in school and graduate with an average below 2.0. That type of pressure can be overwhelming for young people, so make sure you are ready to make this commitment toward obtaining an advanced degree.

Typically, becoming a lawyer involves obtaining a four-year undergraduate degree, attending three years of law school, and passing a bar examination. The requirements for the exam vary by state. According to the *Occupational Outlook Handbook,* there were 195 ABA-accredited law schools in 2006.[16]

One of the women I interviewed, BET executive Debra Lee, held a law degree from Harvard University. As you may recall, Lee left a prestigious law firm to join Black Entertainment Television (BET), to the surprise of many of her colleagues. They thought this was a step backwards for her. However, it does show that the law skills you obtain can be transferred to other nontraditional areas. For Lee, making that career move allowed her to obtain mentors, which resulted in her career advancement and millionaire status when the founder sold the company to Viacom. Data included in the *Occupational Outlook Handbook* shows, however, that the median salaries of graduates nine months after their graduation was highest in private practice ($85,000), followed by business ($60,000), and then government employment ($45,000).[17]

Business

Although there are some amazing business success stories by minority women similar to the ones you heard by Cathy Hughes and Eunice Dudley, there is still a great need for more minority women to consider this profession. I have to point out, however, that this is a profession you should consider only if you do not mind devoting a large part of your waking hours to your business interest. Also, you should not be afraid to keep going until your business is profitable, as most small businesses fail within the first five years of getting started. Remember how tough it was for Cathy Hughes (sleeping on the floor and having her car repossessed, for example) until she was able to get the funding she needed to keep her radio business from shutting down?

The Center for Women's Business Research estimated in 2008 that there were 1.9 million businesses owned by women of color, a figure up from 1.2 million in 2002.[18] That figure represents 20 percent of all privately held women-owned firms in the United States. According to the research, Hispanic and African-American—owned businesses accounted for about one-third of these firms, while Asian- or Pacific-Islander women accounted for 26 percent. Native-American or Alaska-Native women accounted for only 6 percent of these women-owned firms in 2008. Other data in the report show the states with the greatest number of firms for each ethnic group, and the businesses generated $165 billion in revenue.

One of the most important hurdles to overcome in the business world is trying to make the business a success, which includes making it profitable. Researchers Fairlie and Robb of the Massachusetts Institute of Technology recently examined the relationship between race and entrepreneurial success for black, Asian, and white-owned businesses.[19] Specifically, they contend: "Trends in minority business outcomes do not indicate improvement relative to white business outcomes in the past two decades."[20] Also, they found that human and financial capital were important factors in the success of one's business. As you recall from Chapter 2, some social scientists measured human capital in part by one's educational level. They found that firms owned by college graduates had higher sales on the average than those owned by high school dropouts. Similarly, they found that firms whose owners had graduate degrees had higher sales than firms whose owners held undergraduate degrees.

On another note, they found clear relationships between financial capital and business success. Not surprisingly, firms with higher levels of startup capital were more likely to have higher profits and sales and were less likely to fail than their counterparts. They point out, as Cathy Hughes did in an earlier chapter of this book, that lack of access to capital, low levels of personal wealth, and lending discrimination may be especially troubling for minority business owners. Cathy Hughes went to 32 different lenders before she was able to finally receive a much-needed loan for her radio business.

If you are not ready to take the risk often associated with starting your own business, you can examine some of the best jobs for college graduates interested in business and administration identified by Michael Farr in his book *200 Best Jobs for College Graduates*.[21] Examples of occupations in the business field include management analyst, chief executives, budget analyst, auditors, general and operation managers, and private-sector executives. Also, a wealth of information is included about specific job duties for various occupations, annual earning potential, percent growth, and annual openings in that occupational field.

FEDERAL GOVERNMENT

Finally, the federal government continues to be another employer in need of more minorities in top positions. A 2007 General Accounting Office (GAO) report shows the percentage of minorities employed in the U.S. federal government overall and identifies their presence in a select group of 25 government agencies.[22] Those agencies include Agriculture, Agency for International Development, Commerce, Defense, Education, Energy, Environmental Protection, General Services Administration, Health and Human Services, Homeland Security, Housing and Urban Development, Interior, Justice, Labor, National Aeronautics and Space Administration, Nuclear Regulatory Commission, National Science Foundation, Office of Personnel Management, Small Business Administration, Social Security Administration, State, Transportation, Treasury, Veterans Affairs, and Postal Services. There are numerous vacancies in the federal government, with listings covering practically every major discipline. You can find these vacancies on the USA Jobs Web site, www.usajobs.com. You should be aware, however, that as in other industries, some vacancies are tailored toward individuals already in the government, and the position may be open only for a short time because a manager may have someone else in mind. Although these practices are illegal, they can and do happen, as some of the minority women in this book mentioned earlier.

The GAO report shows that minority women had the lowest representation among all government employees. The report presents a variety of comparisons for both 2000 and 2006. However, the latest figures from 2006 give a clear snapshot of where minority women stood. For example, look at their representation in Table 6.3 at the highest rank of the federal government, the senior executive service, followed by the GS 14 and 15 ranks.[23] Typically, federal employees move through a series of successive ranks prior to reaching these higher levels. Table 6.3 shows also that white men and white women had much higher representations than their minority counterparts, with white men holding the bulk of these positions. If you decide to work in the federal government, you can examine similar data for the specific agency of interest to you. As mentioned in earlier chapters you should use your support networks, whether family or friends and professional associates, to help you decide on the agency that best fits your interests.

Table 6.3
Percentage of Employees at the Highest Level of the Federal Government

Employees	SES	GS-15	GS-14
Minority women	5.8	7.6	10.5
Minority men	10.0	11.4	11.7
White women	22.6	22.2	24.2
White men	61.4	58.7	53.4
Total*	99.8	99.9	99.8

*Does not add to 100% due to rounding.
Source: Data from U.S. General Accounting Office, 2007.

The tables in Appendix D show that the representation of minority women ranged from a low of 1.8 percent in the Department of State to a high of almost 25 percent in the Department of Housing and Urban Development agency. The data also show that only five of the 24 federal agencies had 10 percent or more minority women: the Small Business Administration, Social Security Administration, Housing and Urban Development, Agency for International Development, and the Department of Education. Although these numbers are encouraging for these agencies, you still need to do your research and ask tough questions like the ones mentioned in earlier chapters prior to seeking one of these jobs, even if the minority representations looks good.

Two of the women that I interviewed held top jobs in the government that were political appointments rather than career government positions like those mentioned above. Zina Pierre and Rondalyn Kane could only remain in their positions for as long as the then-current United States president was in office. When you accept a political appointment in the federal government, it is unlikely that you will be reappointed when a new president comes into office.

Another important distinction to remember with respect to obtaining a political appointment in the federal service versus a career appointment is this: You do not necessarily have to start at a certain level and work your way up. Neither Pierre nor Kane started out in an entry-level government job like a GS-5 or 7 position. They did not have to move up the career ladder from a GS-9, 11, 12, 13, 14, 15, and then an SES position, as some career service employees may do. Pierre, as you may recall, served as a special assistant to President Bill Clinton in the White House. Kane worked as a deputy director of the Women's Bureau at the Department of Labor. Both were experienced workers already when they sought their political appointments, and their stories should have given you an idea of some of the key ingredients necessary to obtain a political appointment. Typically the process is quite involved and usually requires substantial work experience, political contacts, and support to even be considered for these highly coveted positions. You should know that there is a huge amount of competition from around the country for political appointments in the government or to serve on various boards and commissions. Although this subject would require more details than can be presented here, you will be required to fill out many lengthy forms as part of the background checks conducted to determine your suitability for a political appointment. A great deal of personal information is requested since you serve at the pleasure of the United States president. It should be emphasized, too, that your behavior should reflect positively on the president. No information should be left out, since something embarrassing could emerge that would damage your chances for receiving an appointment. Whether you are interested in a career position or a political appointment, your journey to the top will be equally challenging.

Some Concluding Remarks

I hope the information and the stories shared by the amazing women in this book have inspired and encouraged you to set your career goals high. Just as Debra Lee, Cathy Hughes, Eunice Dudley, Dr. Iris Metts, Dr. Gail Nordmoe, and the others met challenges along the way, they kept the faith, maintained their drive, and built wonderful networks of support to help them promote their career. Take these valuable lessons and chart an exciting career path of your own. You deserve no less.

Notes

1. U.S. Department of Labor, Bureau of Labor Statistics, *Occupational Outlook Handbook 2008–2009* (Indiana: JIST, 2008) and *Encyclopedia of Careers and Vocational Guidance,* 13th ed. (New York: Facts on File, Inc., 2005).

2. Association of American Medical Colleges, *Diversity in the Physician Workforce: Facts and Figures* (Washington, DC: Association of American Medical Colleges, 2006), 18.

3. Ibid.

4. U.S. Department of Labor, Bureau of Labor Statistics, *Occupational Outlook Handbook 2008–2009,* 330.

5. Ibid., 332.

6. Ibid., 330.

7. See, www.womenincongress.house.gov/data/women-of-color.html for additional comments.

8. Colleen Teixeira, "Working in Politics," *Occupational Outlook Quarterly* 52, no. 2 (2008): 1–14.

9. American Association of School Administrators, *State of the American School Superintendency—A Mid Decade Study* (New Jersey: Roman and Littlefield, 2007).

10. Ronald Blakely (Deputy Director of the White House Initiative of Historically Black Colleges and Universities) in discussion with the author, October 2008.

11. Commission on Racial and Ethnic Diversity in the Profession, *Miles to Go: Progress of Minorities in the Legal Profession* (Washington, D.C.: American Bar Association, 2005).

12. Ibid.

13. Ibid.

14. Ibid.

15. Ibid.

16. U.S. Department of Labor, Bureau of Labor Statistics, *Occupational Outlook Handbook 2008–2009,* 228.

17. Ibid., 230.

18. See www.womensbusinessresearch.org and Center for Women's Business Research. That number is based on women owning 51 percent or more of their business rather than the 50 percent ownership requirement calculated by some groups.

19. Robert Fairlie and Alicia Robb, *Race and Entrepreneurial Success: Black, Asian and White-Owned Business in the United States* (Cambridge, MIT Press, 2008).

20. Ibid., 10.

21. Michael Farr (with database work by Laurence Shatkin), *200 Best Jobs for College Graduates* (Indiana: JIST, 2006), 79.

22. See U.S. General Accounting Office, Testimony Before the Subcommittee on Federal Workforce, Postal Service, and the District of Columbia, Committee on Oversight and Government Reform, House of Representatives, Human Capital: Diversity in the Federal SES and the Senior Levels of the U.S. Postal Service, GAO-07-838T (Washington, D.C.: General Accounting Office), 2007.

23. Ibid., 11–34.

Appendix A

METHODOLOGY

The writer interviewed 14 minority women who have made outstanding strides in reaching their career goals. These women were selected because they represented a broad range of fields thought to be of interest to today's young minority women. At the time of the interview, four of the women were business owners and have remained in their chosen field. Cathy Hughes is founder and chairperson of Radio One Inc., the largest African-American owned and operated broadcast company in the United States. Debra Lee is president and chief operating officer of Black Entertainment Television, Holding Inc., a multimedia entertainment corporation. Eunice Dudley is the chief financial officer of Dudley Products Inc., a multimillion-dollar hair care and cosmetics company. Jocelyn Bramble is the publisher of the *Baltimore Times,* the *Prince Georges County Times,* and *Annapolis Times,* with a readership of more than 200,000.

Two of the women held high-level government positions. Zina Pierre was appointed by President Clinton to serve as Special Assistant to the President for Intergovernmental Affairs in the White House. Rondalyn Kane was appointed Deputy Director of the United States Department of Labor's Women's Bureau.

Five of the women were in the educational field. Dr. Iris Metts was Superintendent of Schools for the Prince George's County School System. Dr. Gwen Baker was Director of Social Justice for the American Educational Research Association, a national organization. Dr. Gail Nordmoe was Executive Director of the Richard Green Institute for Teaching and Learning. Dr. Rachel Petty was Vice President for Academic Affairs at the University of the District of Columbia. Dr. Dely Pena was a Senior Program Associate for a large teacher's union.

The remaining three respondents represented a variety of other fields. They included the medical field (Beatrice Muglia, MD), nonprofit organizations (Dr. Jane Smith, Chief Executive Officer of the Business and Professional Women's Association). Andrea Roane is anchor of WUSA news channel 9 in Washington, D.C.

The results of this study are exploratory. The views of the women are not intended to be representative of the larger population of minority women. Rather, the women's responses reflect their views at the time of this study.

Each of the women responded to a 20-minute interview scheduled by telephone or participated in a face-to-face interview. Topics covered included the women's definition of success, factors that they believed were responsible for their career success, obstacles that they encountered in achieving their career goals, and the advice that they would give to minority women today. Seventeen women were originally identified for participation. One, a cabinet-level secretary of a large federal agency, was not available, and the others changed their mind about participating.

ABBREVIATED BIOGRAPHIES OF SUCCESSFUL WOMEN

Catherine Liggins Hughes
Founder and Chairperson of Radio One Inc., Executive Producer of the "Gospel of Music with Jeff Majors," TV Host, TV One

Past Work Experiences
Vice President and General Manager of WYCB, Washington, D.C.
Vice President and General Manager WHUR (Howard University)
Lecturer, School of Communications, Howard University
Executive Director, Project Equality
Administrative Assistant, Howard University, School of Communications

Professional Affiliations
Board member, Baltimore Development Corporation, The Broadcasters Foundation, TV One Television show, Rhythm and Blues Foundation

Community Activities
Sponsor of Piney Woods Summer Camp for Inner City Students
Sponsor of Dream Feast program for the Homeless
Board member, National Urban League
Board member, Maryland African American Museum Corporation

Honors and Awards
Honorary doctorates from such universities as Howard University and Southeastern University in Washington, D.C. and Syracuse University in New York
Recognized as 100 Most Powerful and 100 Most Influential Persons by *Washingtonian* and *Regardies* Magazines
Recognized as one of the 100 who have changed the world by *Essence* Magazine
Lifetime Achievement Award from the Washington Area Broadcasters Association
Golden Mike Award from the Broadcasters Foundation
Inducted into the Maryland Business Hall of Fame
First Annual Black History Hall of Fame Award

National Action Network's Keepers of the Dream Award
Ron Brown Award

Education
College courses in Business Administration (Creighton University and University of Nebraska)

Eunice Mosley Dudley
Chief Financial Officer and Co-Founder and Co-Owner of Dudley Products, Kernersville, North Carolina

Past Work Experiences
Executive Director, Dudley Cosmetology School System
Owner, Fuller Distributorship
Sales Representative, Fuller Products

Community Activities
Bennett College Scholarships, Capital Campaign
Organizer for School of Management for Africa University
Supporter of Black Teenage World Scholarship Pageant
Supporter of North Carolina A&T State University Scholarships

Awards
Honorary Doctor of Humane Letters from Bennett College in North Carolina
Athena Award from Greensboro Chamber of Commerce
Kernersville First Citizens of the Year Award
Crystal Award from Nation Association of Negro Business Women Clubs Inc.
Who's Who Among African Americans

Education
Attended North Carolina A&T State University

Debra Lee
Chairman and CEO of BET Networks

Past Work Experiences
President and CEO, Black Entertainment Television
Attorney, Steptoe and Johnson, Washington, D.C.
Law clerk, Honorable Barrington Parker (dec.)

Professional Affiliations
Women in Cable
The Telecommunications Development Fund
National Symphony Orchestra Board
Board of Directors, BET Holdings

Community Activities
Board of Directors, East Kodak Company, Washington Gas and Light Company, and Kennedy Center's Community board member

Honors and Awards
2000 Tower of Power Trumpet Awards from Turner Broadcasting System
Silver Star Award from the American Women in Radio and Television
Par Excellence Award from *Dollars and Sense* Magazine
Recognized as One of the Hundred Heavy Hitters in Cable by Fox Magazine
Who's Who Among African Americans

Education
J.D. Harvard University Law School
M.A. Harvard University's John F. Kennedy School of Government
B.A. Brown University (Political Science with emphasis in Asian Politics)

Andrea Roane
Anchor and Reporter of 9 Eyewitness News, Washington, D.C.

Past Work Experiences
Host and Chief Correspondent WETA TV's Media Week in Review
Education Reporter WWL-TV, and WYES Television, New Orleans
English Instructor, New Orleans Public Schools
Coordinator of Cultural Services, New Orleans Public Schools

Professional Affiliations
Trustee, Catholic University of America
Lifetime member, NAACP
Board member, George Washington University Mammography Community
Advisory Board

Community Activities
Lifetime member, National Council of Negro Women
Initiated D.C. Breast Cancer Awareness Program—Buddy Check 9

Awards
Outstanding Community Commitment Award from Columbia Hospital for
Women
Leadership Award from American Women in Radio and TV
Outstanding Public Service Award from Chesapeake Associated Press Broadcast-
ing Association
Media Excellence Award from National Foundation of Women Legislators
National Figure/ Outstanding Person Catholic Youth Organization Award
Letter of Recognition, American Association of University Women
Letter of Recognition, National Commission on Working Women
Best of Gannett, Gannett Broadcasting Company

Education
M.A. University of New Orleans (Drama and Communications)
B.A. University of New Orleans (Speech Education)

Gwendolyn Calvert Baker
Retired Educator, Writer, Business Owner, Sarasota, Florida

Past Work Experiences
Director of Social Justice, American Education Research Association
President and Chief Executive Officer, U.S. Committee for UNICEF, New York
National Executive Director, YWCA, New York City
President, New York City Board of Education
Vice President and Dean for Graduate and Children's Program, College of Education, New York City
Chief Minorities and Women's Program, National Institute of Education, Washington, D.C.
Director of Affirmative Action Programs, University of Michigan
Tenured Associate Professor, University of Michigan
Teacher, Michigan Public Schools

Professional Affiliations
Alpha Kappa Alpha Sorority
American Association of University Administrators
American Educational Research Association
Association of Black Women in Higher Education, Advisory Board
International Women's Forum
New York Alliance of Black School Educations
National Association of Women's Deans
New York Coalition of 100 Black Women
Michigan Association for Supervision and Curriculum Development

Community Activities
Personnel Committee Riverside Church
League of Women Voters
Friends of New York City Women's Commission
Mayor's Task Force of Higher Education
City of Ann Arbor Human Relations Commissions
National Council of Negro Women

Honors and Awards
Honorary Doctoral Degrees from eight universities/colleges—The University of Michigan, Chicago State University, Bentley College, Waltham College, Farleigh Dickinson University, Medgar Evers College of the City University of New York, King's Southeastern Massachusetts University
Numerous awards, including August Hawkins Education Service Award
Leadership in Action Award, Women's Action Alliance
Leadership for the Rights of Children, Links
The Nation's 10 Most Admired Women Managers, *Working Women's* Magazine
Recognition of Excellence, National Educator Award

Honorary Co-chair Citizens Ambassador Program of People to People International
Dollars and Sense Award, Salute to America's Top 100 Black Business and Professional Women

Education
Ph.D. University of Michigan (Education)
M.A. University of Michigan (Education Administration)
B.A. University of Michigan (Elementary Education)

Zina Pierre
President and CEO, The Washington Linkage Group Inc., Washington, D.C.

Past Work Experiences
Special Assistant to the President of the United States for Intergovernmental Affairs (Clinton Administration)
Director of the Welfare to Work Initiative, U.S. Small Business Administration
Director of Communications for the Women's Bureau, U.S. Department of Labor
Speechwriter and Senior Media Advisor, U.S. Office of Personnel Management
Journalist for USA Today TV show, America's Most Wanted, Fox Channel Five, News Channel Eight and Sports News Network

Professional Affiliations
Director of the National Black Mayors Corporate Advisory Council
Chair, Board for the National Youth Connection

Community Activities
Vice Chair of "The Future PAC," a national African American Women's Political Action Committee
Board member of Greater Washington Urban League, National Coalition on Black Civic Participation, Black Women's Roundtable, Democratic National Committee Women's Vote Center, Annapolis Children and Family Services, Anne Arundel County Democratic Central Committee
Vice Chair of the African American Leadership Council of the Democratic National Committee

Honors and Awards
Black History Makers Hall of Fame
Citation for Exemplary Public Service
Ron Brown Economic Development Award by the Minority Business Magazine
Outstanding Government Official of the Year by the Minority Business Suppliers
NAACP National Service Award
Delta Sigma Theta Woman of Fortitude Award for Political Involvement
Federally Employed Women Leadership Award

Three time recipient of former Vice President Gore's Heroes of Reinvention Award

National Conference of Mayors Outstanding Service Recognition

Cited in numerous print media such as Essence, Black Enterprise, Sister to Sister, Who's Who in the World, Who's Who in Business

Education

Master's of Divinity Degree from Howard University

B.A. The Catholic University of America (School of Communications)

Jane E. Smith Ed.D.

Executive Director, Spelman College Center for Leadership & Civic Engagement

Past Work Experiences

President, Business and Professional Women's Foundation, Washington, D.C.

President and CEO of the National Council of Negro Women

Director, The Atlanta Project

Managing Director Inroads Atlanta and Inroads Detroit

Assistant to the Vice President for Development, Atlanta University

Assistant to the President, Spelman College

Assistant Professor of Sociology and Director of Freshman Studies

Professional Affiliations

Board of Directors of the Phelps Stokes Fund and Board of Trustees for Knoxville College

Board of Selectors for the American Institute for Public Service

National Women's Business Council

Represented the U.S. as Delegate at the United Nations Beijing Plus Five Conference

Advisory Board of Connect America

Advisory Board of the Black Leadership Forum

National Advisory Board for Reading is Fundamental and Harper-Collins Online Amistad Books Inc.

Links

Delta Sigma Theta Sorority

Community Activities

Served on various city planning commissions and Boards, including:

Leadership Atlanta

Girl Scouts

United Way

Atlanta Empowerment Zone

Bank of America

Prudential Insurance Company

Honors and Awards
Honorary doctorates from Spelman College and Texas College
Recognized as one of American's 50 Most Influential Black Speakers
Emory University Alumni Medal
Johnetta Cole Spelman College Alumni Achievement Award
Recognition from NAACP, YWCA, Allstate Insurance Company
Featured in *Essence, LIFE, Emerge Ebony, Ms.* Magazines, Lifetime TV, C-Span, and CNN.

Education
Ed.D. Harvard University (Social Policy Analysis)
M.A. Emory University (Sociology)
B.A. Spelman College (Sociology)
Iris Metts, Ed.D.
President and CEO, At Choice Solutions Inc.

Past Work Experiences
Chief Education Officer, Mosaica Education Inc.
Superintendent, Prince George's County Maryland Public Schools
Secretary of Education, State of Delaware
Superintendent of Schools, Christina School District of Newark, Delaware
Assistant Superintendent/Acting Supt. Evanston/Skokie School District 65, Evanston, Illinois
Community Relations Administrator, Richmond Public Schools
Director/Principal Marshall-Walker Secondary Complex, Richmond, VA.
Curriculum Specialist/ Assistant Principal, Armstrong High School
Science Department Chairperson, Armstrong High School

Professional Affiliations
Phi Delta Kappa Past President, Delaware Chapter
Association of Supervisors and Curriculum Development
American Association of School Administrators
National Alliance of Black Educators
Urban Superintendent Association of America
Excellence in Economic Education Forum, University of Delaware
Public School Superintendent Association of Maryland

Community Activities
Member of the National Commission on Mathematics and Science Teaching for the 21st Century
Member of ERDI National Education Research Consultants
Governor's Education Improvement Commission, Co-chair Finance Subcommittee and Goals 2000 Committee

Board of Directors member for such groups as Horace Mann League, Project Excellence, Junior Achievement of Delaware and Maryland, Delaware Institute for Arts in Education, Prince George's Chamber of Commerce, Delaware Nature Society, Mid-Atlantic Laboratory for Student Success, Temple University

Awards
Leadership Award, Junior Achievement
Outstanding Community Service Martin Luther King Dinner (Newark NAACP)
Distinguished Leadership Award, AAUW Newark Branch
Delaware Superintendent of the Year
Environmental Education Leadership Award, Delaware Nature Society
Greater Washington Board of Trade Award for Outstanding Service Leadership in the Public Sector

Education
Postdoctoral work at Harvard University (Multicultural Education)
Ed.D. Virginia Polytechnic and State University (Education Administration)
M.A. College of William and Mary (Teaching Physics and Mathematics)
B.S. Hampton University (Physics and Mathematics)

Rachel Petty, Ph.D.
Dean, College of Arts and Sciences, University of the District of Columbia, Washington, D.C.

Past Work Experiences
Acting Vice President for Academic Affairs, University of the District of Columbia (UDC)
Acting Dean, UDC
Assistant Dean, UDC
Chairperson, Department of Psychology
Professor, Department of Psychology
Associate Professor, UDC
Assistant Professor, UDC
Instructor, Federal City College
Adjunct Lecturer, Department of Education, Howard University

Professional Affiliations
American Psychological Association
District of Columbia Psychological Association
American Association of University Women

Community Activities
Maryland Foster Care Review Board

Conference on Developing World Class Educational Standards for the District of Columbia
Lutheran Social Services of the National Capital Area
District of Columbia Child Welfare Consortium

Honors and Awards
Psi Chi Honorary Society in Psychology
Minority Dissertation Fellowship
International Who's Who of American Women
Recognition from the National Association for Equal Opportunity in Higher Education

Education
Ph.D. University of Maryland (Human Development)
M.S. Howard University (General Experimental Psychology)
B.S. Howard University (Psychology)
Deagelia Pena
Director, Pena Education Center Foundation, Parada, Valenzuela City, Philippines

Past Work Experiences
Senior Professional Associate, National Education Association
Associate Director of Research, University of Michigan
Assistant Professor, Wayne State University

Professional Affiliations
American Education Research Association
American Statistical Association
International Association of Statistical Computing
International Association of Survey Statisticians
Fulbright Alumni Association

Community Activities
Former Trustee Gibson School for the Gifted and Talented
Judge of the Annual Science Fairs Washington Statistical Society
Superintendent's Advisory Committee on Minority Student Achievement

Honors and Awards
International Who's Who in Education
First Place Civil Service Examination for Statisticians
College Scholar, M.A. Statistics Program University of the Philippines

Education
Ph.D. University of Michigan (Educational Research)
M.S. University of Michigan (Mathematics)

M.A. University of the Philippines
B.S. St. Theresa's College, Manila Philippines

Gail Nordmoe, Ed.D.
Assistant Professor, Sacred Heart University, College of Education and Health Professions, Fairfield, Connecticut

Past Work Experiences
Executive Director, Richard Green Institute for Teaching and Learning
Assistant Superintendent of Curriculum and Instruction for Danbury Connecticut Public Schools and for Cambridge, Massachusetts Public Schools

Professional Affiliations
National Council of Supervisors of Mathematics
American Association of University Women
American Education Research Association
Black Women in Higher Education
Association for Supervision and Curriculum Development
Community Activities
Former member of Board of Directors of Danbury Hospital
Founding member of Minnesota chapter of Black Women in Higher Education
Writing Children's Literature to Foster Cross Cultural Understanding

Honors and Awards
City of Detroit Mayor's Award for Community Service
Inspirational Women's Award for 2002 from Business and Professional Women's Association
Women of Distinction Award from Mayor of the City of Danbury
Resolution from the Board of Directors of Danbury Hospital for Efforts to Improve Health Care in the Community

Education
Ed. D. Wayne State University (Curriculum Development)
M.A. Wayne State University (Mathematics Education)
B.A. University of Illinois (Sociology)

Jocelyn "Joy" Bramble
Publisher, Baltimore Times, Annapolis Times, Shore Times, Prince Georges County Times, Baltimore, MD

Past Work Experiences
Principal, All Saints Secondary School
Antigua, West Indies
Owner, two neighborhood grocery stores in Baltimore, MD

Professional Affiliations
Serves on numerous boards and commissions, including University of Maryland School of Medicine Board of Trustees, Maryland Education, Maryland Education Coalition, and Goodwill Industries

Community Activities
Founder of the Times Community Services Foundation, which sponsors an annual family expo, a black men's festival, and a yearly women's forum
Founding member, Montserrat Historical Trust, the island's first museum

Honors and Awards
Who's Who Among Women Businesspersons

Education
B.A. Queen's University, Kingston Ontario (Professional teaching certificate, University of Calgary)

Beatrice Muglia, M.D.
Staff Pathologist, Bon Secours Hospital, Gross Pointe, Michigan
Past Work Experience
Staff Pathologist
Wheeling Hospital
Wheeling, West Virginia

Professional Affiliations
American Society of Clinical Pathologists
College of American Pathologists
International Academy of Pathology
Community Activities

Honors and Awards
Fellowship, Case Western University, University Hospital Health System

Education
M.D. Michigan State University
B.A. University of Michigan

Rondalyn Kane
Director, Strategy and Innovation, NCB Capital Impact

Past Work Experiences
Deputy Director, Women's Bureau
U.S. Department of Labor
Executive Director, Congressional Black Caucus Foundation
Lobbyist, Service Employees International Union
Assoc. Staff Member, U.S. House Rules Committee, U.S. House of Representatives

Community Activities
Designed and delivered workshops for Harvard Women and Power Workshop, Harvard University
Designed Emerging Leaders Workshop, University of Maryland
Conducted workshop for Whose Plan Is It?, African American Women's Resource Center

Education
B.A. Political Science, Univ. of Maryland, Baltimore County
M.P.A. University of Southern California
Graduate Level Certificates: Transformational Leadership, Psychological Dimensions of Management Excellence, Organizational Development, Georgetown University

Professional Seminars/Speaking Engagements
2008. Women and Power Conference (Workshop on transformational leadership) at Harvard University
2008. Whose Plan Is It? (Workshop on core values, leadership, and life planning) at the African American Women's Resource Center
2008. Emerging Leaders Workshop. (Workshop on leadership) at the University of Maryland
2007. International Career Advancement Program (ICAP) Annual Conference (Seminar on successfully transitioning from public-sector to private-sector careers with a global organization) involving an audience of 100 global professionals and mid-level managers.
2004. Harvard Women and Power Workshop. (Workshop designed to handle difficult performance management and diversity communications) involving an audience of 50 female global business owners and senior executives
2003. Harvard Women and Power Workshop. (Workshop on values-based leadership)

INTERVIEW SCHEDULE

Name of Interviewer_____
Date: _____
Name of Interviewee_____
Successful Women Study

"Good morning. I am _____. This interview is conducted to provide ideas to young minority women on how to become successful in obtaining their career goals. Additionally, we hope to obtain feedback later from those reading the results of this study in order to improve our recommendations to minority women. Your participation will be crucial to thousands of young women across the country.

I want to start by asking you how do you define success? (PROBE ON MONEY, KNOWLEDGE, POWER, ANYTHING THE INDIVIDUAL ASPIRES FOR, INTERVIEWER TAKE COMPLETE NOTES.)

What factors do you consider most responsible for your success today? (INTERVIEWER PROBE FOR SUPPORTIVE FAMILY MEMBERS, HAVING A MENTOR, GOING TO AN IVY LEAGUE SCHOOL...LIST IN ORDER GIVEN TO YOU.)

First: _____
Second_____
Third_____

If you can attribute your success to somebody in achieving your position today, tell me how much is the percentage contribution of these persons? (PERCENT SHOULD ADD UP TO 100.)

Yourself_____percent
Mother_____percent
Father_____percent
Teacher_____percent
Mentor_____ percent
Your employer_____ percent
Other_____percent (specify)

At what point in your life did you become aware of your desire to become successful? (PROBE ON, SINCE I WAS FIVE, HIGH SCHOOL, COLLEGE ETC. WHAT BROUGHT THIS TO MIND?)

At what point did you start working toward this goal? (PROBE ON SINCE HIGH SCHOOL, COLLEGE ETC.)

Thinking back to when you were a teenager, what occupations or careers most interested you? What did you want to be?

Tell me about your first professional job. (PROBE TO FIND OUT, HOW DID YOU FIND OUT ABOUT IT? WHAT DID YOU LIKE MOST ABOUT THE JOB? WHAT DID YOUR LIKE LEAST? HOW WOULD YOU DESCRIBE YOUR SUPERVISOR? COWORKERS?)

Did this job match your college study or previous academic program?

What other jobs did you hold prior to the one that you currently hold? (List LAST JOB HELD IF PERSON HAS RETIRED.)

Thinking about your last position, who was most helpful to you when you needed professional help on the job?

When you needed to talk about problems that came your way, who offered their support? (PROBE: WHY DO YOU THINK YOU WERE SUPPORTED, WERE THEY IN A MANAGERIAL OR STAFF POSITION?)

What do you consider your most significant obstacles to reaching your career goals or did success come easily?

How would you describe the organizational culture for the last place where you worked? (PROBE TO FIND OUT: SUPPORTIVE OF WOMEN, GRIEVANCE PROCESS, ENFORCEMENT OF RACE AND SEX DISCRIMINATION POLICIES, PROMOTIONAL PRACTICES, etc.)

If you could start over, would you choose the same line of professional work? (PROBE FOR OTHER INCLINATIONS THEY DID NOT PURSUE.)

What do you think is the greatest obstacle confronting young minority professional women today?

What advice would you give to these young women who would like to achieve the financial success that you have today?

Tell me a little about your family life. (PROBE: HOW MANY BROTHERS AND SISTERS DO YOU HAVE? WHAT DO THEY DO NOW FOR A LIVING? WHAT TYPE OF WORK DID YOUR PARENTS OR CARETAKERS DO FOR A LIVING? DID YOU ENJOY YOUR CHILDHOOD YEARS? WHAT ABOUT YOUR COLLEGE YEARS?)

INTERVIEWER: ASK AND CIRCLE ONE:

Race: BLACK FILIPINO JAPANESE AMERICAN INDIAN

Marital status: MARRIED SINGLE WIDOWED DIVORCED

Age range: Under 40 41-50 51-60 OVER 60

THANKS SO MUCH FOR YOUR TIME AND WE WILL SEND YOU THE RESULTS OF OUR STUDY.

Minority Representation in the Senior Executive Service (SES)

The following agency acronyms are used in the Appendix D tables: Agriculture, Agency for International Development (AID), Commerce, Defense, Education, Energy, Environmental Protection (EPA), General Services Administration (GSA), Health and Human Services (HHS), Homeland Security (DHS), Housing and Urban Development (HUD), Interior (DOI), Justice (DOJ), Labor, National Aeronautics and Space Administration (NASA), Nuclear Regulatory Commission (NRC), National Science Foundation (NSF), Office of Personnel Management (OPM), Small Business Administration (SBA), Social Security Administration (SSA), State, Transportation, Treasury, Veterans (VA).

Table D.1
Percentage of Employees in the Senior Executive Service of the Federal Government (SES)*

	EPA	GSA	HHS	DHS	HUD	DOI	DOJ
Minority Women	6.2	5.6	9.9	3.1	24.4	9.3	3.8
Minority Men	9.6	5.6	12.3	9.5	15.9	16.3	14.0
White Women	31.5	21.1	33.0	22.9	13.4	23.3	18.0
White Men	52.7	67.6	44.7	64.5	46.3	51.1	64.0

*Note: Totals may not add to 100 percent due to rounding. Source of data: U.S. General Accounting Office, 2007.

Table D.2

Percentage of Employees in the Senior Executive Service of the Federal Government (SES)*

	NRC	NSF	OPM	SBA	SSA	NASA
Minority Women	3.9	5.1	7.5	11.4	15.3	6.0
Minority Men	11.2	10.3	10.0	25.7	14.6	9.9
White Women	16.4	37.2	22.5	20.0	24.3	17.1
White Men	68.4	47.4	60.0	42.9	45.8	67.0

*Note: Totals may not add to 100 percent due to rounding. Source of data: U.S. General Accounting Office, 2007.

Table D.3

Percentage of Employees in the Senior Executive Service of the Federal Government (SES)*

	Agriculture	AID	Commerce	Defense	Education	Energy
Minority Women	6.4	17.8	3.8	2.5	13.7	5.4
Minority Men	12.1	11.8	8.9	5.4	11.0	9.2
White Women	24.8	29.4	24.0	18.5	26.0	16.8
White Men	56.8	41.2	63.3	73.3	49.3	68.6

*Note: Totals may not add to 100 percent due to rounding. Source of data: U.S. General Accounting Office, 2007.

Table D.4

Percentage of Employees in the Senior Executive Service of the Federal Government (SES)*

	State	Transportation	Treasury	Labor	VA
Minority Women	1.8	6.0	6.3	9.9	2.6
Minority Men	4.4	9.9	12.3	10.7	11.8
White Women	29.8	28.6	28.3	23.1	21.4
White Men	64.0	55.5	52.8	56.2	63.8

*Note: Totals may not add to 100 percent due to rounding. Source of data: U.S. General Accounting Office, 2007.

Descriptions of the Highest-Paid Occupations (From the *Occupational Outlook Handbook*, 2008–2009)

Top Executives

Significant Points

- Keen competition is expected because the prestige and high pay of these jobs attract a large number of applicants.
- Top executives are among the highest paid workers; however, long hours, considerable travel, and intense pressure to succeed are common.
- The formal education and experience of top executives vary as widely as the nature of their responsibilities.

Nature of the Work

All organizations have specific goals and objectives that they strive to meet. Top executives devise strategies and formulate policies to ensure that these objectives are met. Although they have a wide range of titles—such as chief executive officer, chief operating officer, board chair, president, vice president, school superintendent, county administrator, or tax commissioner—all formulate policies and direct the operations of businesses and corporations, public sector organizations, nonprofit institutions, and other organizations.

A corporation's goals and policies are established by the chief executive officer in collaboration with other top executives, who are overseen by a board of directors. In a large corporation, the chief executive officer meets frequently with subordinate executives to ensure that operations are conducted in accordance with these policies. The chief executive officer of a corporation retains overall accountability; however, a chief operating officer may be delegated several responsibilities, including the authority to oversee executives who direct the activities of various departments and implement the organization's policies on a day-to-day basis. In publicly held and nonprofit corporations, the board of directors ultimately is accountable for the success or failure of the enterprise, and the chief executive officer reports to the board.

In addition to being responsible for the operational success of a company, top executives also are increasingly being held accountable for the accuracy of their financial reporting, particularly among publicly traded companies. For example, recently enacted legislation contains provisions for corporate governance, internal control, and financial reporting.

The nature of the responsibilities of other high-level executives depends on the size of the organization. In small organizations, such as independent retail stores or small manufacturers, a partner, owner, or general manager often is responsible for purchasing, hiring, training, quality control, and day-to-day supervisory duties. In large organizations, the duties of executives are highly specialized. Some managers, for instance, are responsible for the overall performance of one aspect of the organization, such as manufacturing, marketing, sales, purchasing, finance, personnel, training, administrative services, computer and information systems, property management, transportation, or legal services. (Some of these and other management occupations are discussed elsewhere in this section of the Handbook.)

Chief financial officers direct the organization's financial goals, objectives, and budgets. They oversee the investment of funds and manage associated risks, supervise cash management activities, execute capital-raising strategies to support a firm's expansion, and deal with mergers and acquisitions.

Chief information officers are responsible for the overall technological direction of their organizations. They are increasingly involved in the strategic business plan of a firm as part of the executive team. To perform effectively, they also need knowledge of administrative procedures, such as budgeting, hiring, and supervision. These managers propose budgets for projects and programs and make decisions on staff training and equipment purchases. They hire and assign computer specialists, information technology workers, and support personnel to carry out specific parts of the projects. They supervise the work of these employees, review their output, and establish administrative procedures and policies. Chief information officers also provide organizations with the vision to master information technology as a competitive tool.

Chief executives have overall responsibility for the operation of their organizations. Working with executive staff, they set goals and arrange programs to attain these goals. Executives also appoint department heads, who manage the employees who carry out programs. Chief executives also oversee budgets and ensure that resources are used properly and that programs are carried out as planned.

Chief executive officers carry out a number of other important functions, such as meeting with staff and board members to determine the level of support for proposed programs. Chief executive officers in government often nominate citizens to boards and commissions, encourage business investment, and promote economic development in their communities. To do all of these varied tasks effectively, chief executives rely on a staff of highly skilled personnel. Executives who control small companies, however, often do this work by themselves.

General and operations managers plan, direct, or coordinate the operations of companies or public and private sector organizations. Their duties include formulating policies, managing daily operations, and planning the use of materials and human resources, but are too diverse and general in nature to be classified in any one area of management or administration, such as personnel, purchasing, or administrative services. In some organizations, the duties of general and operations managers may overlap the duties of chief executive officers.

Work environment. Top executives typically have spacious offices and numerous support staff. General managers in large firms or nonprofit organizations usually have comfortable offices close to those of the top executives to whom they report. Long hours, including evenings and weekends, are standard for most top executives and general managers, although their schedules may be flexible.

Substantial travel between international, national, regional, and local offices to monitor operations and meet with customers, staff, and other executives often is required of managers and executives. Many managers and executives also attend meetings and conferences sponsored by various associations. The conferences provide an opportunity to meet with prospective donors, customers, contractors, or government officials and allow managers and executives to keep abreast of technological and managerial innovations.

In large organizations, job transfers between local offices or subsidiaries are common for persons on the executive career track. Top executives are under intense pressure to succeed; depending on the organization, this may mean earning higher profits, providing better service, or attaining fundraising and charitable goals. Executives in charge of poorly performing organizations or departments usually find their jobs in jeopardy.

TRAINING, OTHER QUALIFICATIONS, AND ADVANCEMENT

The formal education and experience required by top executives vary as widely as their responsibilities do, but many of these workers have at least a bachelor's degree and considerable experience.

Education and training. Many top executives have a bachelor's or graduate degree in business administration, liberal arts, or a more specialized discipline. The specific degree required often depends on the type of organization for which they work. College presidents, for example, typically have a doctorate in the field in which they originally taught, and school superintendents often have a master's degree in education administration. (For information on lower-level managers in educational services, see the Handbook statement on education administrators.) A brokerage office manager needs a strong background in securities and finance, and department store executives generally have extensive experience in retail trade.

Some top executives in the public sector have a background in public administration or liberal arts. Others might have a more specific background related to their jobs. For example, a health commissioner might have a graduate degree in health services administration or business administration. (For information on lower-level managers in health services, see the Handbook statement on medical and health services managers.)

Many top executive positions are filled from within the organization by promoting experienced, lower-level managers when an opening occurs. In industries such as retail trade or transportation, for instance, it is possible for individuals without a college degree to work their way up within the company and become managers. However, many companies prefer that their top executives have extensive managerial experience and, therefore, hire individuals who have been managers in other organizations.

Other qualifications. Top executives must have highly developed personal skills. An analytical mind able to quickly assess large amounts of information and data is very important, as is the ability to consider and evaluate the relationships between numerous factors. Top executives also must be able to communicate clearly and persuasively. For managers to succeed they need other important qualities as well, including leadership, self-confidence, motivation, decisiveness, flexibility, sound business judgment, and determination.

Certification and advancement. Advancement may be accelerated by participation in company training programs that impart a broader knowledge of company policy and operations. Managers also can help their careers by becoming familiar with the latest developments in management techniques at national or local training programs sponsored by various industry and trade associations. To facilitate their promotion to an even higher level, managers who have experience in a particular field, such as accounting or engineering, may attend executive development programs geared towards their background.

Participation in conferences and seminars can expand knowledge of national and international issues influencing the organization and can help the participants develop a network of useful contacts. For example, the Institute of

Certified Professional Managers offers the Certified Manager (CM) credential, which is earned by completing training and passing an exam. The certification is held by individuals at all experience levels, from those seeking to enter management to those who are already senior executives. Certification is not necessary for advancement but may be helpful in developing and demonstrating valuable management skills.

General managers may advance to a top executive position, such as executive vice president, in their own firm or they may take a corresponding position in another firm. They may even advance to peak corporate positions such as chief operating officer or chief executive officer. Chief executive officers often become members of the board of directors of one or more firms, typically as a director of their own firm and often as chair of its board of directors. Some top executives establish their own firms or become independent consultants.

EMPLOYMENT

Top executives held about 2.1 million jobs in 2006. Employment by detailed occupation was distributed as follows:

General and operations managers	1,720,000
Chief executives	402,000

Top executives are found in every industry, but service-providing industries, including government, employed over 3 out of 4 top executives.

JOB OUTLOOK

Employment of top executives is projected to have little or no change. Keen competition for jobs is expected because of the prestige and high pay of these positions.

Employment change. Employment of top executives—including chief executives, general and operations managers, and legislators—is expected to grow 2 percent from 2006 to 2016. Because top managers are essential to the success of any organization, their jobs are unlikely to be automated or offshored to other countries. Some top executive jobs may be eliminated through industry consolidation, as upper management is streamlined after mergers and acquisitions. Employment of top executives is not as sensitive to growth in business as employment in many other occupations. As a business grows, the number of top executives changes little relative to the total number of employees. Therefore, top executives are not expected to experience as much employment growth as workers in the occupations they oversee.

Projected employment growth of top executives varies by industry. For example, employment growth is expected to grow faster than average in professional, scientific, and technical services and about as fast as the average in administrative and support services. However, employment is projected to decline in some manufacturing industries.

Job prospects. Keen competition is expected for top executive positions because the prestige and high pay attract a large number of qualified applicants. Because this is a large occupation, numerous openings will occur each year as executives transfer to other positions, start their own businesses, or retire. However, many executives who leave their jobs transfer to other executive positions, a pattern that tends to limit the number of job openings for new entrants to the occupation.

Experienced managers whose accomplishments reflect strong leadership qualities and the ability to improve the efficiency or competitive position of an organization will have the best opportunities. In an increasingly global economy, experience in international economics, marketing, information systems, and knowledge of several languages also may be beneficial.

EARNINGS

Top executives are among the highest paid workers in the U.S. economy. However, salary levels vary substantially depending on the level of managerial responsibility; length of service; and type, size, and location of the firm. For example, a top manager in a very large corporation can earn significantly more than a counterpart in a small firm.

Median annual earnings of wage and salary general and operations managers in May 2006 were $85,230. The middle 50 percent earned between $58,230 and $128,580. Because the specific responsibilities of general and operations managers vary significantly within industries, earnings also tend to vary considerably. Median annual earnings in the industries employing the largest numbers of general and operations managers were:

Architectural, engineering, and related services	$113,280
Management of companies and enterprises	$105,130

Median annual earnings of wage and salary chief executives in May 2006 were greater than $145,600; some chief executives of large companies earn hundreds of thousands to over a million dollars annually, although salaries vary substantially by type and level of responsibilities and by industry.

In addition to salaries, total compensation often includes stock options and other performance bonuses. The use of executive dining rooms and company aircraft and cars, expense allowances, and company-paid insurance premiums and physical examinations also are among benefits commonly enjoyed by top executives in private industry. A number of chief executive officers also are provided with company-paid club memberships and other amenities.

RELATED OCCUPATIONS

Top executives plan, organize, direct, control, and coordinate the operations of an organization and its major departments or programs. The members of the board of directors and lower-level managers also are involved in these activities. Many other management occupations have similar responsibilities; however, they are concentrated in specific industries or are responsible for a specific department within an organization. A few examples are administrative services managers; education administrators; financial managers; food service managers; and advertising, marketing, promotions, public relations, and sales managers. Legislators oversee their staffs and help set public policies in Federal, State, and local governments.

SOURCES OF ADDITIONAL INFORMATION

Disclaimer: Links to non-BLS Internet sites are provided for your convenience and do not constitute an endorsement.

For more information on top executives, including educational programs and job listings, contact:

American Management Association, 1601 Broadway, 6th Floor, New York, NY 10019. Internet: http://www.amanet.org

National Management Association, 2210 Arbor Blvd., Dayton, OH 45439. Internet: http://www.nma1.org

For more information on executive financial management careers, contact:

Financial Executives International, 200 Campus Dr., P.O. Box 674, Florham Park, NJ 07932. Internet: http://www.financialexecutives.org
Financial Management Association International, College of Business Administration, University of South Florida, 4202 East Fowler Ave., BSN 3331, Tampa, FL 33620. Internet: http://www.fma.org

For information about management skills development, including the Certified Manager (CM) credential, contact:

Institute for Certified Professional Managers, 1598 S. Main St., Harrisonburg, VA 22801. Internet: http://www.icpm.biz

Source: Bureau of Labor Statistics, U.S. Department of Labor, Occupational Outlook Handbook, 2008–09 Edition, Top Executives, on the Internet at http://www.bls.gov/oco/ocos012.htm (visited November 09, 2008).

ECONOMISTS

Significant Points

- Slower than average job growth is expected as firms increasingly employ workers with titles that reflect specialized duties rather than the general title of economist.
- Job seekers with a background in economics should have opportunities in various occupations.
- Candidates who hold a master's or Ph.D. degree in economics will have the best employment prospects and advancement opportunities.
- Quantitative skills are important in all economics specialties.

NATURE OF THE WORK

Economists study how society distributes resources, such as land, labor, raw materials, and machinery, to produce goods and services. They may conduct research, collect and analyze data, monitor economic trends, or develop forecasts. Economists research a wide variety of issues including energy costs, inflation, interest rates, exchange rates, business cycles, taxes, and employment levels, among others.

Economists develop methods for obtaining the data they need. For example, sampling techniques may be used to conduct a survey and various mathematical modeling techniques may be used to develop forecasts. Preparing reports, including tables and charts, on research results also is an important part of an economist's job. Presenting economic and statistical concepts in a clear and meaningful way is particularly important for economists whose research is intended for managers and others who do not have a background in economics. Some economists also perform economic analysis for the media.

Many economists specialize in a particular area of economics, although general knowledge of basic economic principles is essential. Microeconomists study the supply and demand decisions of individuals and firms, such as how profits can be maximized and the quantity of a good or service that consumers will demand at a certain price. Industrial economists or organizational economists study the market structure of particular industries in terms of the number of competitors within those industries and examine the market decisions of competitive firms and monopolies. These economists also may be concerned with antitrust policy and its impact on market structure. Macroeconomists study historical trends in the whole economy and forecast future trends in areas such as unemployment, inflation, economic growth, productivity, and investment. Doing similar work as macroeconomists are monetary economists or financial economists, who study the money and banking system and the effects of changing interest rates. International economists study international financial markets, exchange rates, and the effects of various trade policies such as tariffs. Labor economists or demographic economists study the supply and demand for labor and the determination of wages. These economists also try to explain the reasons for unemployment and the effects of changing demographic trends, such as an aging population and increasing immigration, on labor markets. Public finance economists are involved primarily in studying the role of the government in the economy and the effects of tax cuts, budget deficits, and welfare policies. Econometricians investigate all areas of economics and apply mathematical techniques such as calculus, game theory, and regression analysis to their research. With these techniques, they formulate economic models that help explain economic relationships and that can be used to develop forecasts about business cycles, the effects of a specific rate of inflation on the economy, the effects of tax legislation on unemployment levels, and other economic phenomena.

Many economists apply these areas of economics to health, education, agriculture, urban and regional economics, law, history, energy, the environment, or other issues. Most economists are concerned with practical applications of economic policy. Economists working for corporations are involved primarily in microeconomic issues, such as forecasting consumer demand and sales of the firm's products. Some analyze their competitors' growth and market share and advise their company on how to handle the competition. Others monitor legislation passed by Congress, such as environmental and worker safety regulations, and assess how the new laws will affect the corporation. Corporations with many international branches or subsidiaries might employ economists to monitor the economic situations in countries where they do business or to provide a risk assessment of a country into which the company is considering expanding.

Economists working in economic consulting or research firms sometimes perform the same tasks as economists working for corporations. However, economists in consulting firms also perform much of the macroeconomic analysis and forecasting conducted in the United States. These economists collect data on various economic indicators, maintain databases, analyze historical trends, and develop models to forecast growth, inflation, unemployment, or interest rates. Their analyses and forecasts are frequently published in newspapers and journal articles.

Another large employer of economists is the government. Economists in the Federal Government administer most of the surveys and collect the majority of the economic data about the United States. For example, economists in the U.S. Department of Commerce collect and analyze data on the production, distribution, and consumption of commodities produced in the United States and overseas, and economists employed by the U.S. Department of Labor collect and analyze data on the domestic economy, including data on prices, wages, employment, productivity, and safety and health.

Economists who work for government agencies also assess economic conditions in the United States or abroad to estimate the effects of specific changes in legislation or public policy. Government economists advise policy makers in areas such as the deregulation of industries, the effects of changes to Social Security, the effects of tax cuts on the budget deficit, and the effectiveness of imposing tariffs on imported goods. An economist working in state or local government might analyze data on the growth of school-age or prison populations and on employment and unemployment rates in order to project future spending needs.

Work environment. Economists have structured work schedules. They often work alone, writing reports, preparing statistical charts, and using computers, but they also may be an integral part of a research team. Most work under pressure of deadlines and tight schedules, which may require overtime. Their routine may be interrupted by special requests for data and by the need to attend meetings or conferences. Frequent travel may be necessary.

Training, Other Qualifications, and Advancement

Some entry-level positions for economists are available to those with a bachelor's degree, but higher degrees are required for many positions. Prospective economists need good quantitative skills.

Education and training. A master's or Ph.D. degree in economics is required for many private sector economist jobs and for advancement to more responsible positions. In the Federal Government, candidates for entry-level economist positions must have a bachelor's degree with a minimum of 21 semester hours of economics and 3 hours of statistics, accounting, or calculus.

Economics includes numerous specialties at the graduate level, such as econometrics, international economics, and labor economics. Students should select graduate schools that are strong in the specialties that interest them. Some schools help graduate students find internships or part-time employment in government agencies, economic consulting or research firms, or financial institutions before graduation.

Undergraduate economics majors can choose from a variety of courses, ranging from microeconomics, macroeconomics, and econometrics to more philosophical courses, such as the history of economic thought. Because of the importance of quantitative skills to economists, courses in mathematics, statistics, econometrics, sampling theory and survey design, and computer science are extremely helpful.

Whether working in government, industry, research organizations, or consulting firms, economists with a bachelor's degree usually qualify for entry-level positions as a research assistant, for administrative or management trainee positions, or for various sales jobs. A master's degree usually is required to qualify for more responsible research and administrative positions. A Ph.D. is necessary for top economist positions in many organizations. Also, many corporation and government executives have a strong background in economics.

Aspiring economists should gain experience gathering and analyzing data, conducting interviews or surveys, and writing reports on their findings while in college. This experience can prove invaluable later in obtaining a full-time position in the field because much of the economist's work, especially in the beginning, may center on these duties. With experience, economists eventually are assigned their own research projects. Related job experience, such as work as a stock or bond trader, might be advantageous.

Other qualifications. Those considering careers as economists should be able to pay attention to details because much time is spent on precise data analysis. Candidates also should have strong computer and quantitative skills and be able to perform complex research. Patience and persistence are necessary qualities, given that economists must spend long hours on independent study and problem solving. Good communication skills also are useful, as economists must be able to present their findings, both orally and in writing, in a clear, concise manner.

Advancement. With experience or an advanced degree, economists may advance into positions of greater responsibility, including administration and independent research.

Many people with an economics background become teachers. (See the statement on teachers—postsecondary elsewhere in the Handbook.) A master's degree usually is the minimum requirement for a job as an instructor in a junior or community college. In most colleges and universities, however, a Ph.D. is necessary for appointment as an instructor. A Ph.D. and extensive publications in academic journals are required for a professorship, tenure, and promotion.

EMPLOYMENT

Economists held about 15,000 jobs in 2006. Government employed 52 percent of economists, in a wide range of agencies, with 32 percent in Federal Government and 20 percent in State and local government. The remaining jobs were spread throughout private industry, particularly in scientific research and development services and management, scientific, and technical consulting services. A number of economists combine a full-time job in government, academia, or business with part-time or consulting work in another setting.

Employment of economists is concentrated in large cities. Some work abroad for companies with major international operations, for U.S. Government agencies, and for international organizations, such as the World Bank, International Monetary Fund, and United Nations.

In addition to the previously mentioned jobs, economists hold faculty positions in colleges and universities. Economics faculties have flexible work schedules and may divide their time among teaching, research, consulting, and administration. These workers are counted as postsecondary teachers, not economists.

Job outlook. Employment of economists is expected to grow about as fast as the average for all occupations. The demand for workers who have knowledge and skill in economics is projected to grow faster, but these workers are often in occupations other than economist. Job prospects will be best for those with graduate degrees in economics.

Employment change. Employment of economists is expected to grow seven percent from 2006 to 2016, about as fast as the average for all occupations. Demand for economic analysis should grow, but the increase in the number of economist jobs will be tempered as firms hire workers for more specialized jobs with specialized titles. Many workers with economic backgrounds will work in related occupations with more specific job titles, such as financial analyst, market analyst, public policy consultant, researcher or research assistant, and purchasing manager. Overall employment growth also will be slowed because of the relatively high number of economists employed in slow growing or declining government sectors. Employment in Federal government agencies is expected to decrease, and employment in State and local government is expected to grow more slowly than employment in the private sector.

Employment growth should be fastest in private industry, especially in management, scientific, and technical consulting services. Rising demand for economic analysis in virtually every industry should stem from the growing complexity of the global economy, the effects of competition on businesses, and increased reliance on quantitative methods for analyzing and forecasting business, sales, and other economic trends. Some corporations choose to hire economic consultants to fill these needs, rather than keeping an economist on staff. This practice should result in more economists being employed in consulting services.

Job prospects. In addition to job openings from growth, the need to replace experienced workers who transfer to other occupations or who retire or leave the labor force for other reasons will create openings for economists.

Individuals with a background in economics should have opportunities in various occupations. As indicated earlier, some examples of job titles often held by those with an economics background are financial analyst, market analyst, public policy consultant, researcher or research assistant, and purchasing manager.

People who have a master's or Ph.D. degree in economics, who are skilled in quantitative techniques and their application to economic modeling and forecasting, and who also have good communications skills, should have the best job opportunities. Like those in many other disciplines, some economists leave the occupation to become professors, but competition for tenured teaching positions is expected to be keen.

Bachelor's degree holders may face competition for the limited number of economist positions for which they qualify. However, they will qualify for a number of other positions that can use their economic knowledge. Many graduates with bachelor's degrees will find jobs in industry and business as management or sales trainees. Bachelor's degree holders with good quantitative skills and a strong background in mathematics, statistics, survey design, and computer science also may be hired as researchers. Some will find jobs in government.

Candidates who meet State certification requirements may become high school economics teachers. The demand for secondary school economics teachers is expected to grow, as economics becomes an increasingly important and popular course. (See the statement on teachers—preschool, kindergarten, elementary, middle, and secondary elsewhere in the Handbook.)

EARNINGS

Median annual wage and salary earnings of economists were $77,010 in May 2006. The middle 50 percent earned between $55,740 and $103,500. The lowest 10 percent earned less than $42,280, and the highest 10 percent earned more than $136,550.

In the Federal Government, the starting salary for economists having a bachelor's degree was $35,752 in 2007. Those having a master's degree could qualify for positions with an annual salary of $43,731. Those with a Ph.D. could begin at $52,912, and some individuals with experience and an advanced degree could start at $63,417. Starting salaries were higher in selected geographical areas where the prevailing local pay was higher. The average annual salary for economists employed by the Federal Government was $94,098 a year in 2007.

Economists are concerned with understanding and interpreting financial matters, among other subjects. Other occupations in this area include accountants and auditors; actuaries; budget analysts; cost estimators; financial analysts and personal financial advisors; financial managers; insurance underwriters; loan officers; and purchasing managers, buyers, and purchasing agents. Economists also rely heavily on quantitative analysis, as do mathematicians, statisticians, and operations research analysts. Other occupations involved in market research and data collection are management analysts and market and survey researchers. Economists also study consumer behavior, similar to the work of sociologists.

SOURCES OF ADDITIONAL INFORMATION

Disclaimer:Links to non-BLS Internet sites are provided for your convenience and do not constitute an endorsement.

For information on careers in business economics, contact:

National Association for Business Economics, 1233 20th St. NW., Suite 505, Washington, DC 20036.

Information on obtaining positions as economists with the Federal Government is available from the Office of Personnel Management through USAJOBS, the Federal Government's official employment information system.

This resource for locating and applying for job opportunities can be accessed through the Internet at http://www.usajobs.opm.gov or through an interactive voice response telephone system at (703) 724-1850 or TDD (978) 461-8404. These numbers are not toll free, and charges may result. For advice on how to find and apply for Federal jobs, see the Occupational Outlook Quarterly article "How to get a job in the Federal Government," online at http://www.bls.gov/opub/ooq/2004/summer/art01.pdf.

Source: Bureau of Labor Statistics, U.S. Department of Labor, Occupational Outlook Handbook, 2008-09 Edition, Economists, on the Internet at http://www.bls.gov/oco/ocos055.htm (visited November 09, 2008).

PHYSICIANS AND SURGEONS

Significant Points

- Many physicians and surgeons work long, irregular hours; more than one-third of full-time physicians worked 60 hours or more a week in 2006.
- Acceptance to medical school is highly competitive.
- Formal education and training requirements are among the most demanding of any occupation, but earnings are among the highest.
- Job opportunities should be very good, particularly in rural and low-income areas.

NATURE OF THE WORK

Physicians and surgeons diagnose illnesses and prescribe and administer treatment for people suffering from injury or disease. Physicians examine patients, obtain medical histories, and order, perform, and interpret diagnostic tests. They counsel patients on diet, hygiene, and preventive health care.

There are two types of physicians: M.D.—Doctor of Medicine—and D.O.—Doctor of Osteopathic Medicine. M.D.s also are known as allopathic physicians. While both M.D.s and D.O.s may use all accepted methods of treatment, including drugs and surgery, D.O.s place special emphasis on the body's musculoskeletal system, preventive medicine, and holistic patient care. D.O.s are most likely to be primary care specialists although they can be found in all specialties. About half of D.O.s practice general or family medicine, general internal medicine, or general pediatrics.

Physicians work in one or more of several specialties, including, but not limited to, anesthesiology, family and general medicine, general internal medicine, general pediatrics, obstetrics and gynecology, psychiatry, and surgery.

Anesthesiologists focus on the care of surgical patients and pain relief. Like other physicians, they evaluate and treat patients and direct the efforts of their staffs. Through continual monitoring and assessment, these critical care specialists are responsible for maintenance of the patient's vital life functions—heart rate, body temperature, blood pressure, breathing—during surgery. They also work outside of the operating room, providing pain relief in the intensive care unit, during labor and delivery, and for those who suffer from chronic pain. Anesthesiologists confer with other physicians and surgeons about appropriate treatments and procedures before, during, and after operations.

Family and general practitioners often provide the first point of contact for people seeking health care, by acting as the traditional family doctor. They assess and treat a wide range of conditions, from sinus and respiratory infections to broken bones. Family and general practitioners typically have a base of regular, long-term patients. These doctors refer patients with more serious conditions to specialists or other health care facilities for more intensive care.

General internists diagnose and provide nonsurgical treatment for a wide range of problems that affect internal organ systems, such as the stomach, kidneys, liver, and digestive tract. Internists use a variety of diagnostic techniques to treat patients through medication or hospitalization. Like general practitioners, general internists commonly act as primary care specialists. They treat patients referred from other specialists, and, in turn they refer patients to other specialists when more complex care is required.

General pediatricians care for the health of infants, children, teenagers, and young adults. They specialize in the diagnosis and treatment of a variety of ailments specific to young people and track patients' growth to adulthood. Like most physicians, pediatricians work with different health care workers, such as nurses and other physicians, to assess and treat children with various ailments. Most of the work of pediatricians involves treating day-to-day illnesses—minor injuries, infectious diseases, and immunizations—that are common to children, much as a general practitioner treats adults. Some pediatricians specialize in pediatric surgery or serious medical conditions, such as autoimmune disorders or serious chronic ailments.

Obstetricians and gynecologists (OB/GYNs) specialize in women's health. They are responsible for women's general medical care, and they also provide care related to pregnancy and the reproductive system. Like general practitioners, OB/GYNs attempt to prevent, diagnose, and treat general health problems, but they focus on ailments specific to the female anatomy, such as cancers of the breast or cervix, urinary tract and pelvic disorders, and hormonal disorders. OB/GYNs also specialize in childbirth, treating and counseling women throughout their pregnancy, from giving prenatal diagnoses to assisting with delivery and providing postpartum care.

Psychiatrists are the primary caregivers in the area of mental health. They assess and treat mental illnesses through a combination of psychotherapy, psychoanalysis, hospitalization, and medication. Psychotherapy involves regular discussions with patients about their problems; the psychiatrist helps them find solutions through changes in their behavioral patterns, the exploration of their past experiences, or group and family therapy sessions. Psychoanalysis involves long-term psychotherapy and counseling for patients. In many cases, medications are administered to correct chemical imbalances that cause emotional problems. Psychiatrists also may administer electroconvulsive therapy to those of their patients who do not respond to, or who cannot take, medications.

Surgeons specialize in the treatment of injury, disease, and deformity through operations. Using a variety of instruments, and with patients under anesthesia, a surgeon corrects physical deformities, repairs bone and tissue after injuries, or performs preventive surgeries on patients with debilitating diseases or disorders. Although a large number perform general surgery, many surgeons choose to specialize in a specific area. One of the most prevalent specialties is orthopedic surgery: the treatment of the musculoskeletal system. Others include neurological surgery (treatment of the brain and nervous system), cardiovascular surgery, otolaryngology (treatment of the ear, nose, and throat), and plastic or reconstructive surgery. Like other physicians, surgeons also examine patients, perform and interpret diagnostic tests, and counsel patients on preventive health care.

Other physicians and surgeons work in a number of other medical and surgical specialists, including allergists, cardiologists, dermatologists, emergency physicians, gastroenterologists, ophthalmologists, pathologists, and radiologists.

Work environment. Many physicians—primarily general and family practitioners, general internists, pediatricians, OB/GYNs, and psychiatrists—work in small private offices or clinics, often assisted by a small staff of nurses and other administrative personnel. Increasingly, physicians are practicing in groups or health care organizations that provide backup coverage and allow for more time off. Physicians in a group practice or health care organization often work as part of a team that coordinates care for a number of patients; they are less independent than the solo practitioners of the past. Surgeons and anesthesiologists usually work in well-lighted, sterile environments while performing surgery and often stand for long periods. Most work in hospitals or in surgical outpatient centers.

Many physicians and surgeons work long, irregular hours. Over one-third of full-time physicians and surgeons worked 60 hours or more a week in 2006. Only 8 percent of all physicians and surgeons worked part-time, compared with 15 percent for all occupations. Physicians and surgeons must travel frequently between office and hospital to care for their patients. While on call, a physician will deal with many patients' concerns over the phone and make emergency visits to hospitals or nursing homes.

TRAINING, OTHER QUALIFICATIONS, AND ADVANCEMENT

The common path to practicing as a physician requires 8 years of education beyond high school and 3 to 8 additional years of internship and residency. All States, the District of Columbia, and U.S. territories license physicians.

Education and training. Formal education and training requirements for physicians are among the most demanding of any occupation—4 years of undergraduate school, 4 years of medical school, and 3 to 8 years of internship and residency, depending on the specialty selected. A few medical schools offer combined undergraduate and medical school programs that last 6 years rather than the customary 8 years.

Premedical students must complete undergraduate work in physics, biology, mathematics, English, and inorganic and organic chemistry. Students also take courses in the humanities and the social sciences. Some students volunteer at local hospitals or clinics to gain practical experience in the health professions.

The minimum educational requirement for entry into medical school is 3 years of college; most applicants, however, have at least a bachelor's degree, and many have advanced degrees. There are 146 medical schools in the United States—126 teach allopathic medicine and award a Doctor of Medicine (M.D.) degree; 20 teach osteopathic medicine and award the Doctor of Osteopathic Medicine (D.O.) degree.

Acceptance to medical school is highly competitive. Applicants must submit transcripts, scores from the Medical College Admission Test, and letters of recommendation. Schools also consider an applicant's character, personality, leadership qualities, and participation in extracurricular activities. Most schools require an interview with members of the admissions committee.

Students spend most of the first 2 years of medical school in laboratories and classrooms, taking courses such as anatomy, biochemistry, physiology, pharmacology, psychology, microbiology, pathology, medical ethics, and laws governing medicine. They also learn to take medical histories, examine patients, and diagnose illnesses. During their last 2 years, students work with patients under the supervision of experienced physicians in hospitals and clinics, learning acute, chronic, preventive, and rehabilitative care. Through rotations in internal medicine, family practice, obstetrics and gynecology, pediatrics, psychiatry, and surgery, they gain experience in the diagnosis and treatment of illness.

Following medical school, almost all M.D.s enter a residency—graduate medical education in a specialty that takes the form of paid on-the-job training, usually in a hospital. Most D.O.s serve a 12-month rotating internship after graduation and before entering a residency, which may last 2 to 6 years.

A physician's training is costly. According to the Association of American Medical Colleges, in 2004 more than 80 percent of medical school graduates were in debt for educational expenses.

Licensure and certification. All States, the District of Columbia, and U.S. territories license physicians. To be licensed, physicians must graduate from an accredited medical school, pass a licensing examination, and complete 1 to 7 years of graduate medical education. Although physicians licensed in one State usually can get a license to practice in another without further examination, some States limit reciprocity. Graduates of foreign medical schools generally can qualify for licensure after passing an examination and completing a U.S. residency.

M.D.s and D.O.s seeking board certification in a specialty may spend up to 7 years in residency training, depending on the specialty. A final examination immediately after residency or after 1 or 2 years of practice also is necessary for certification by a member board of the American Board of Medical Specialists (ABMS) or the American Osteopathic Association (AOA). The ABMS represents 24 boards related to medical specialties ranging from allergy and immunology to urology. The AOA has approved 18 specialty boards, ranging from anesthesiology to surgery. For certification in a subspecialty, physicians usually need another 1 to 2 years of residency.

Other qualifications. People who wish to become physicians must have a desire to serve patients, be self-motivated, and be able to survive the pressures and long hours of medical education and practice. Physicians also must have a good bedside manner, emotional stability, and the ability to make decisions in emergencies. Prospective physicians must be willing to study throughout their career to keep up with medical advances.

Advancement. Some physicians and surgeons advance by gaining expertise in specialties and subspecialties and by developing a reputation for excellence among their peers and patients. Many physicians and surgeons start their own practice or join a group practice. Others teach residents and other new doctors, and some advance to supervisory and managerial roles in hospitals, clinics, and other settings.

Employment

Physicians and surgeons held about 633,000 jobs in 2006; approximately 15 percent were self-employed. About half of wage–and-salary physicians and surgeons worked in offices of physicians, and 18 percent were employed by hospitals. Others practiced in Federal, State, and local governments, including colleges, universities, and professional schools; private colleges, universities, and professional schools; and outpatient care centers.

According to 2005 data from the American Medical Association (AMA), about one half of physicians in patient care were in primary care, but not in a subspecialty of primary care, as follows:

Percent distribution of active physicians in patient care by specialty, 2005

Primary care	40.4
Family medicine and general practice	12.3
Internal medicine	15.0
Obstetrics & gynecology	5.5
Pediatrics	7.5
Specialties	59.6
Anesthesiology	5.2
Psychiatry	5.1
Surgical specialties, selected	10.8
All other specialties	38.5

Source: American Medical Association, Physician Characteristics and Distribution in the US, 2007

A growing number of physicians are partners or wage-and-salary employees of group practices. Organized as clinics or as associations of physicians, medical groups can more easily afford expensive medical equipment, can share support staff, and benefit from other business advantages.

According to the AMA, the New England and Middle Atlantic States have the highest ratio of physicians to population; the South Central and Mountain States have the lowest. D.O.s are more likely than M.D.s to practice in small cities and towns and in rural areas. M.D.s tend to locate in urban areas, close to hospitals and education centers.

JOB OUTLOOK

Employment of physicians and surgeons is expected to grow faster than the average for all occupations. Job opportunities should be very good, especially for physicians and surgeons willing to practice in specialties—including family practice, internal medicine, and OB/GYN—or in rural and low-income areas where there is a perceived shortage of medical practitioners.

Employment change. Employment of physicians and surgeons is projected to grow 14 percent from 2006 to 2016, faster than the average for all occupations. Job growth will occur because of continued expansion of health care related industries. The growing and aging population will drive overall growth in the demand for physician services, as consumers continue to demand high levels of care using the latest technologies, diagnostic tests, and therapies.

Demand for physicians' services is highly sensitive to changes in consumer preferences, health care reimbursement policies, and legislation. For example, if changes to health coverage result in consumers facing higher out-of-pocket costs, they may demand fewer physician services. Patients relying more on other health care providers—such as physician assistants, nurse practitioners, optometrists, and nurse anesthetists—also may temper demand for physician services. In addition, new technologies will increase physician productivity. These technologies include electronic medical records, test and prescription orders, billing, and scheduling.

Job prospects. Opportunities for individuals interested in becoming physicians and surgeons are expected to be very good. In addition to job openings from employment growth, numerous openings will result from the need to replace physicians and surgeons who retire over the 2006-16 decade.

Unlike their predecessors, newly trained physicians face radically different choices of where and how to practice. New physicians are much less likely to enter solo practice and more likely to take salaried jobs in group medical practices, clinics, and health networks.

Reports of shortages in some specialties, such as general or family practice, internal medicine, and OB/GYN, or in rural or low-income areas should attract new entrants, encouraging schools to expand programs and hospitals to increase available residency slots. However, because physician training is so lengthy, employment change happens gradually. In the short term, to meet increased demand, experienced physicians may work longer hours, delay retirement, or take measures to increase productivity, such as using more support staff to provide services. Opportunities should be particularly good in rural and low-income areas, as some physicians find these areas unattractive because of less control over work hours, isolation from medical colleagues, or other reasons.

EARNINGS

Earnings of physicians and surgeons are among the highest of any occupation. The Medical Group Management Association's Physician Compensation and Production Survey, reports that median total compensation for physicians in 2005 varied by specialty, as follows. Total compensation for physicians reflects the amount reported as direct compensation for tax purposes, plus all voluntary salary reductions. Salary, bonus and incentive payments, research stipends, honoraria, and distribution of profits were included in total compensation.

Median Compensation for Physicians, 2005

Specialty	Less Than Two Years in Specialty	Over One Year in Specialty
Anesthesiology	$259,948	$321,686
Surgery: General	228,839	282,504
Obstetrics/gynecology: General	203,270	247,348
Psychiatry: General	173,922	180,000
Internal medicine: General	141,912	166,420
Pediatrics: General	132,953	161,331
Family practice (without obstetrics)	137,119	156,010

Source: Medical Group Management Association, Physician Compensation and Production Report, 2005

Self-employed physicians—those who own or are part owners of their medical practice—generally have higher median incomes than salaried physicians. Earnings vary according to number of years in practice, geographic region, hours worked, skill, personality, and professional reputation. Self-employed physicians and surgeons must provide for their own health insurance and retirement.

RELATED OCCUPATIONS

Physicians work to prevent, diagnose, and treat diseases, disorders, and injuries. Other health care practitioners who need similar skills and who exercise critical judgment include chiropractors, dentists, optometrists, physician assistants, podiatrists, registered nurses, and veterinarians.

SOURCES OF ADDITIONAL INFORMATION

Disclaimer:Links to non-BLS Internet sites are provided for your convenience and do not constitute an endorsement.

For a list of medical schools and residency programs, as well as general information on premedical education, financial aid, and medicine as a career, contact:

American Association of Colleges of Osteopathic Medicine, 5550 Friendship Blvd., Suite 310, Chevy Chase, MD 20815. Internet: http://www.aacom.org

Association of American Medical Colleges, Section for Student Services, 2450 N St. NW., Washington, DC 20037. Internet: http://www.aamc.org/students

For general information on physicians, contact:

American Medical Association, 515 N. State St., Chicago, IL 60610. Internet: http://www.ama-assn.org

American Osteopathic Association, Department of Communications, 142 East Ontario St., Chicago, IL 60611. Internet: http://www.osteopathic.org

For information about various medical specialties, contact:

American Academy of Family Physicians, Resident Student Activities Department, 11400 Tomahawk Creek Pkwy., Leawood, KS 66211. Internet: http://fmignet.aafp.org

American Academy of Pediatrics, 141 Northwest Point Blvd., Elk Grove Village, IL 60007. Internet: http://www.aap.org

American Board of Medical Specialties, 1007 Church St., Suite 404, Evanston, IL 60201. Internet: http://www.abms.org

American College of Obstetricians and Gynecologists, 409 12th St. SW., P.O. Box 96920, Washington, DC 20090. Internet: http://www.acog.org

American College of Physicians, 190 North Independence Mall West, Philadelphia, PA 19106. Internet: http://www.acponline.org

American College of Surgeons, Division of Education, 633 North Saint Clair St., Chicago, IL 60611. Internet: http://www.facs.org

American Psychiatric Association, 1000 Wilson Blvd., Suite 1825, Arlington, VA 22209. Internet: http://www.psych.org

American Society of Anesthesiologists, 520 N. Northwest Hwy., Park Ridge, IL 60068. Internet: http://www.asahq.org/career/homepage.htm

Information on Federal scholarships and loans is available from the directors of student financial aid at schools of medicine. Information on licensing is available from State boards of examiners.

Source: Bureau of Labor Statistics, U.S. Department of Labor, Occupational Outlook Handbook, 2008-09 Edition, Physicians and Surgeons, on the Internet at http://www.bls.gov/oco/ocos074.htm (visited November 09, 2008).

ENGINEERING AND NATURAL SCIENCES MANAGERS

Significant Points

- Most engineering and natural sciences managers have formal education and work experience as engineers, scientists, or mathematicians.
- Projected employment growth for engineering and natural sciences managers is closely related to growth in employment of the engineers and scientists they supervise and the industries in which they work.
- Opportunities will be best for workers with strong communication and business management skills.

NATURE OF THE WORK

Engineering and natural sciences managers plan, coordinate, and direct research, design, and production activities. They may supervise engineers, scientists, and technicians, along with support personnel. These managers use their knowledge of engineering and natural sciences to oversee a variety of activities. They determine scientific and technical goals within broad outlines provided by top executives, who are discussed elsewhere in the Handbook. These goals may include improving manufacturing processes, advancing scientific research, or developing new products. Managers make detailed plans to accomplish these goals. For example, they may develop the overall concepts of a new product or identify technical problems preventing the completion of a project.

To perform effectively, these managers also must apply knowledge of administrative procedures, such as budgeting, hiring, and supervision. They propose budgets for projects and programs and determine staff, training, and equipment needs. They hire and assign scientists, engineers, and support personnel to carry out specific parts of each project. They also supervise the work of these employees, check the technical accuracy of their work and the soundness of their methods, review their output, and establish administrative procedures and policies—including environmental standards, for example.

In addition, these managers use communication skills extensively. They spend a great deal of time coordinating the activities of their unit with those of other units or organizations. They confer with higher levels of management; with financial, production, marketing, and other managers; and with contractors and equipment and materials suppliers.

Engineering managers may supervise people who design and develop machinery, products, systems, and processes. They might also direct and coordinate production, operations, quality assurance, testing, or maintenance in industrial plants. Many are plant engineers, who direct and coordinate the design, installation, operation, and maintenance of equipment and machinery in industrial plants. Others manage research and development teams that produce new products and processes or improve existing ones.

Natural sciences managers oversee the work of life and physical scientists, including agricultural scientists, chemists, biologists, geologists, medical scientists, and physicists. These managers direct research and development projects and coordinate activities such as testing, quality control, and production. They may work on basic research projects or on commercial activities. Science managers sometimes conduct their own research in addition to managing the work of others.

Work environment. Engineering and natural sciences managers spend most of their time in an office. Some managers, however, also may work in laboratories, where they may be exposed to the same conditions as research scientists, or in industrial plants, where they may be exposed to the same conditions as production workers. Most managers work at least 40 hours a week and may work much longer on occasion to meet project deadlines. Some may experience considerable pressure to meet technical or scientific goals on a short deadline or within a tight budget.

TRAINING, OTHER QUALIFICATIONS, AND ADVANCEMENT

Strong technical knowledge is essential for engineering and natural sciences managers, who must understand and guide the work of their subordinates and explain the work in nontechnical terms to senior management and potential customers. Therefore, most managers have formal education and work experience as an engineer, scientist, or mathematician.

Education and training. These managers usually have education similar to that of the workers they supervise. Most engineering managers, for example, begin their careers as engineers, after completing a bachelor's degree in the field. Many engineers gain business management skills by completing a master's degree in engineering management (MEM) or business administration (MBA). Employers often pay for such training. In large firms, some courses required in these degree programs may be offered onsite. Typically, engineers who prefer to manage in technical areas pursue an MEM, and those interested in less technical management earn an MBA.

Similarly, many science managers begin their careers as scientists, such as chemists, biologists, geologists, or mathematicians. Most scientists and mathematicians engaged in basic research have a Ph.D. degree; some who work in applied research and other activities may have a bachelor's or master's degree. Graduate programs allow scientists to augment their undergraduate training with instruction in other fields, such as management or computer technology. Natural science managers interested in more technical management may earn traditional master's or Ph.D. degrees in natural sciences or master's degrees in science that incorporate business management skills. Those interested in more general management may pursue an MBA. Given the rapid pace of scientific developments, science managers must continuously upgrade their knowledge.

Other qualifications. Engineering and natural sciences managers must be specialists in the work they supervise. To advance to these positions, engineers and scientists generally must gain experience and assume management responsibility. To fill management positions, employers seek engineers and scientists who possess administrative and communication skills in addition to technical knowledge in their specialty. In fact, because engineering and natural sciences managers must effectively lead groups and coordinate projects, they usually need excellent communication and administrative skills.

Advancement. Engineering and natural sciences managers may advance to progressively higher leadership positions within their disciplines. Some may become managers in nontechnical areas such as marketing, human resources, or sales. In high technology firms, managers in nontechnical areas often must possess the same specialized knowledge as do managers in technical areas. For example, employers in an engineering firm may prefer to hire experienced engineers as sales workers because the complex services offered by the firm can be marketed only by someone with specialized engineering knowledge. Such sales workers could eventually advance to jobs as sales managers.

EMPLOYMENT

Engineering and natural sciences managers held about 228,000 jobs in 2006. Manufacturing industries employed 38 percent of engineering and natural sciences managers. Manufacturing industries with the largest employment are those which produce computer and electronic equipment and those which produce transportation equipment, including aerospace products and parts. Another 31 percent worked in professional, scientific, and technical services industries, primarily for firms providing architectural, engineering, and related services and firms providing scientific research and development services. Other large employers include Federal, State, and local government agencies.

JOB OUTLOOK

Employment of engineering and natural sciences managers is projected to grow about as fast as the average for all occupations, similar to the growth rate of engineers and life and physical scientists. Opportunities will be best for workers with strong communication and business management skills.

Employment change. Employment of engineering and natural sciences managers is expected to grow 8 percent over the 2006-16 decade, about as fast as the average for all occupations. Projected employment growth for engineering and natural sciences managers should be in line with growth of the engineers and scientists they supervise and the industries in which they work. Because many employers find it more efficient to contract engineering and science work to specialty firms, there should be strong demand for engineering managers in the scientific research and development services industry and for both engineering and natural science managers in the architectural, engineering, and related services industry.

Job prospects. Opportunities for engineering managers should be better in rapidly growing areas of engineering—such as environmental and biomedical engineering—than in more slowly growing areas—such as electronics and materials engineering. Opportunities for natural sciences managers should likewise be best in the rapidly growing medical and environmental sciences. (See the statements on engineers and life and physical scientists elsewhere in the Handbook.) Engineers and scientists with advanced technical knowledge and strong communication skills will be in the best position to become managers. Because engineering and natural sciences managers are involved in the financial, production, and marketing activities of their firm, business management skills are also advantageous for those seeking management positions. In addition to those openings resulting from employment growth, job openings will result from the need to replace managers who retire or move into other occupations.

EARNINGS

Earnings for engineering and natural sciences managers vary by specialty and by level of responsibility. Median annual earnings of wage and salary engineering managers were $105,430 in May 2006. The middle 50 percent earned between $84,090 and $130,170. Median annual earnings in the industries employing the largest numbers of engineering managers were:

Semiconductor and other electronic component manufacturing	$120,740
Federal executive branch	116,140
Navigational, measuring, electromedical, and control instruments manufacturing	115,150
Aerospace product and parts manufacturing	111,020
Engineering services	103,570

Median annual earnings of wage and salary natural sciences managers were $100,080 in May 2006. The middle 50 percent earned between $77,320 and

$130,900. Median annual earnings in the industries employing the largest numbers of natural sciences managers were:

Research and development in the physical, engineering, and life sciences	$120,780
Pharmaceutical and medicine manufacturing	111,070
Federal executive branch	96,100
Architectural, engineering, and related services	88,990
State government	65,570

In addition, engineering and natural sciences managers, especially those at higher levels, often receive more benefits—such as expense accounts, stock option plans, and bonuses—than do nonmanagerial workers in their organizations.

RELATED OCCUPATIONS

The work of engineering and natural sciences managers is closely related to that of engineers; mathematicians; and physical and life scientists, including agricultural and food scientists, atmospheric scientists, biological scientists, conservation scientists and foresters, chemists and materials scientists, environmental scientists and hydrologists, geoscientists, medical scientists, and physicists and astronomers. It also is related to the work of other managers, especially top executives.

SOURCES OF ADDITIONAL INFORMATION

Disclaimer:Links to non-BLS Internet sites are provided for your convenience and do not constitute an endorsement.

For information about a career as an engineering and natural sciences manager, contact the sources of additional information for engineers, life scientists, and physical scientists that are listed at the end of statements on these occupations elsewhere in the Handbook.

Additional information on science and engineering master's degrees is available from:

Commission on Professionals in Science and Technology, 1200 New York Ave. NW., Suite 113, Washington, DC 20005. Internet: http://www.science masters.org

To learn more about managing scientists and engineers in research and development, see the Occupational Outlook Quarterly article, "Careers for scientists—and others—in scientific research and development," online at http://www .bls.gov/opub/ooq/2005/summer/art04.htm and in print at many libraries and career centers.

Source: Bureau of Labor Statistics, U.S. Department of Labor, Occupational Outlook Handbook, 2008-09 Edition, Engineering and Natural Sciences Managers, on the Internet at http://www.bls.gov/oco/ocos009.htm (visited November 09, 2008).

DENTISTS

Significant Points

- Most dentists are solo practitioners.
- Dentists usually complete at least 8 years of education beyond high school.
- Average employment growth will generate some job openings, but most openings will result from the need to replace the large number of dentists expected to retire.
- Job prospects should be good.

NATURE OF THE WORK

Dentists diagnose and treat problems with teeth and tissues in the mouth, along with giving advice and administering care to help prevent future problems. They provide instruction on diet, brushing, flossing, the use of fluorides, and other aspects of dental care. They remove tooth decay, fill cavities, examine x rays, place protective plastic sealants on children's teeth, straighten teeth, and repair fractured teeth. They also perform corrective surgery on gums and supporting bones to treat gum diseases. Dentists extract teeth and make models and measurements for dentures to replace missing teeth. They also administer anesthetics and write prescriptions for antibiotics and other medications.

Dentists use a variety of equipment, including x-ray machines, drills, mouth mirrors, probes, forceps, brushes, and scalpels. They wear masks, gloves, and safety glasses to protect themselves and their patients from infectious diseases.

Dentists in private practice oversee a variety of administrative tasks, including bookkeeping and the buying of equipment and supplies. They may employ and supervise dental hygienists, dental assistants, dental laboratory technicians, and receptionists. (These occupations are described elsewhere in the Handbook.)

Most dentists are general practitioners, handling a variety of dental needs. Other dentists practice in any of nine specialty areas. Orthodontists, the largest group of specialists, straighten teeth by applying pressure to the teeth with braces or retainers. The next largest group, oral and maxillofacial surgeons, operates on the mouth and jaws. The remainder may specialize as pediatric dentists (focusing on dentistry for children); periodontists (treating gums and bone supporting the teeth); prosthodontists (replacing missing teeth with permanent fixtures, such as crowns and bridges, or with removable fixtures such as dentures); endodontists (performing root canal therapy); public health dentists (promoting good dental health and preventing dental diseases within the community); oral pathologists (studying oral diseases); or oral and maxillofacial radiologists (diagnosing diseases in the head and neck through the use of imaging technologies).

Work environment. Most dentists are solo practitioners, meaning that they own their own businesses and work alone or with a small staff. Some dentists have partners, and a few work for other dentists as associate dentists.

Most dentists work 4 or 5 days a week. Some work evenings and weekends to meet their patients' needs. The number of hours worked varies greatly among dentists. Most full-time dentists work between 35 and 40 hours a week. However, others, especially those who are trying to establish a new practice, work more. Also, experienced dentists often work fewer hours. It is common for dentists to continue in part-time practice well beyond the usual retirement age.

TRAINING, OTHER QUALIFICATIONS, AND ADVANCEMENT

All 50 States and the District of Columbia require dentists to be licensed. To qualify for a license in most States, candidates must graduate from an accredited dental school and pass written and practical examinations.

Education and training. In 2006, there were 56 dental schools accredited by the American Dental Association's (ADA's) Commission on Dental Accreditation. Dental schools require a minimum of 2 years of college-level predental education prior to admittance. Most dental students have at least a bachelor's degree before entering dental school, although a few applicants are accepted to dental school after 2 or 3 years of college and complete their bachelor's degree while attending dental school.

High school and college students who want to become dentists should take courses in biology, chemistry, physics, health, and mathematics. College undergraduates planning on applying to dental school are required to take many science courses. Because of this, some choose a major in a science, such as biology or chemistry, while others take the required science coursework while pursuing a major in another subject.

All dental schools require applicants to take the Dental Admissions Test (DAT). When selecting students, schools consider scores earned on the DAT, applicants' grade point averages, and information gathered through recommendations and interviews. Competition for admission to dental school is keen.

Dental school usually lasts 4 academic years. Studies begin with classroom instruction and laboratory work in science, including anatomy, microbiology, biochemistry, and physiology. Beginning courses in clinical sciences, including laboratory techniques, are also completed. During the last 2 years, students treat patients, usually in dental clinics, under the supervision of licensed dentists. Most dental schools award the degree of Doctor of Dental Surgery (DDS). Others award an equivalent degree, Doctor of Dental Medicine (DMD).

Some dental school graduates work for established dentists as associates for 1 to 2 years to gain experience and save money to equip an office of their own. Most dental school graduates, however, purchase an established practice or open a new one immediately after graduation.

Licensure. Licensing is required to practice as a dentist. In most States, licensure requires passing written and practical examinations in addition to having a degree from an accredited dental school. Candidates may fulfill the written part of the State licensing requirements by passing the National Board Dental Examinations. Individual States or regional testing agencies administer the written or practical examinations.

In 2006, 17 States licensed or certified dentists who intended to practice in a specialty area. Requirements include 2 to 4 years of postgraduate education and, in some cases, the completion of a special State examination. Most State licenses permit dentists to engage in both general and specialized practice.

Other qualifications. Dentistry requires diagnostic ability and manual skills. Dentists should have good visual memory, excellent judgment regarding space, shape, and color, a high degree of manual dexterity, and scientific ability. Good business sense, self-discipline, and good communication skills are helpful for success in private practice.

Advancement. Dentists who want to teach or conduct research usually spend an additional 2 to 5 years in advanced dental training, in programs operated by dental schools or hospitals. A recent survey by the American Dental Education Association showed that 11 percent of new graduates enrolled in postgraduate training programs to prepare for a dental specialty.

EMPLOYMENT

Dentists held about 161,000 jobs in 2006. Employment was distributed among general practitioners and specialists as follows:

Dentists, general	136,000
Orthodontists	9,200
Oral and maxillofacial surgeons	7,700
Prosthodontists	1,000
Dentists, all other specialists	6,900

About one third of dentists were self-employed and not incorporated. Almost all dentists work in private practice. According to the ADA, about 3 out of 4 dentists in private practice are sole proprietors, and 1 in 7 belongs to a partnership. A few salaried dentists work in hospitals and offices of physicians.

JOB OUTLOOK

Average employment growth will generate some job openings, but most openings will result from the need to replace the large number of dentists expected to retire. Job prospects should be good as new dentists take over established practices or start their own.

Employment change. Employment of dentists is projected to grow nine percent through 2016, about as fast as the average for all occupations. The demand for dental services is expected to continue to increase. The overall population is growing, particularly the number of older people, which will increase the demand for dental care. As members of the baby-boom generation advance into middle age, a large number will need complicated dental work, such as bridges. In addition, elderly people are more likely to retain their teeth than were their predecessors, so they will require much more care than in the past. The younger generation will continue to need preventive checkups despite an overall increase in the dental health of the public over the last few decades. Recently, some private insurance providers have increased their dental coverage. If this trend continues, those with new or expanded dental insurance will be more likely to visit a dentist than in the past. Also, while they are currently a small proportion of dental expenditures, cosmetic dental services, such as fitting braces for adults as well as children and providing teeth-whitening treatments, have become increasingly popular.

However, employment of dentists is not expected to keep pace with the increased demand for dental services. Productivity increases from new technology, as well as having dental hygienists and assistants perform some tasks, will allow dentists to perform more work than they have in the past. As their practices expand, dentists are likely to hire more hygienists and dental assistants to handle routine services.

Dentists will increasingly provide care and instruction aimed at preventing the loss of teeth, rather than simply providing treatments such as fillings. Improvements in dental technology also will allow dentists to offer more effective and less painful treatment to their patients.

Job prospects. As an increasing number of dentists from the baby-boom generation reach retirement age, many of them will retire or work fewer hours. However, the number of applicants to, and graduates from, dental schools has increased in recent years. Therefore, younger dentists will be able to take over the work from older dentists who retire or cut back on hours, as well as provide dental services to accommodate the growing demand.

Demand for dental services tends to follow the business cycle, primarily because these services usually are paid for either by the patient or by private insurance companies. As a result, during slow times in the economy, demand for dental services can decrease; dentists may have difficulty finding employment, or if already in an established practice, they may work fewer hours because of reduced demand.

EARNINGS

Median annual earnings of salaried dentists were $136,960 in May 2006. Earnings vary according to number of years in practice, location, hours worked, and specialty. Self-employed dentists in private practice tend to earn more than do salaried dentists.

Dentists who are salaried often receive benefits paid by their employer, with health insurance and malpractice insurance being among the most common. However, like other business owners, self-employed dentists must provide their own health insurance, life insurance, retirement plans, and other benefits.

RELATED OCCUPATIONS

Dentists examine, diagnose, prevent, and treat diseases and abnormalities. Chiropractors, optometrists, physicians and surgeons, podiatrists, psychologists, and veterinarians do similar work.

SOURCES OF ADDITIONAL INFORMATION

Disclaimer:Links to non-BLS Internet sites are provided for your convenience and do not constitute an endorsement.

For information on dentistry as a career, a list of accredited dental schools, and a list of State boards of dental examiners, contact:

American Dental Association, Commission on Dental Accreditation, 211 E. Chicago Ave., Chicago, IL 60611. Internet: http://www.ada.org

For information on admission to dental schools, contact:

American Dental Education Association, 1400 K St. NW., Suite 1100, Washington, DC 20005. Internet: http://www.adea.org

Persons interested in practicing dentistry should obtain the requirements for licensure from the board of dental examiners of the State in which they plan to work.

To obtain information on scholarships, grants, and loans, including Federal financial aid, prospective dental students should contact the office of student financial aid at the schools to which they apply.

Source: Bureau of Labor Statistics, U.S. Department of Labor, Occupational Outlook Handbook, 2008-09 Edition, Dentists, on the Internet at http://www.bls.gov/oco/ocos072.htm (visited November 09, 2008).

LAWYERS

Significant Points

- About 27 percent of lawyers are self-employed, either as partners in law firms or in solo practices.

- Formal requirements to become a lawyer usually include a 4-year college degree, 3 years of law school, and passing a written bar examination; however, some requirements may vary by State.
- Competition for admission to most law schools is intense.
- Competition for job openings should be keen because of the large number of students graduating from law school each year.

NATURE OF THE WORK

The legal system affects nearly every aspect of our society, from buying a home to crossing the street. Lawyers form the backbone of this system, linking it to society in numerous ways. They hold positions of great responsibility and are obligated to adhere to a strict code of ethics.

Lawyers, also called attorneys, act as both advocates and advisors in our society. As advocates, they represent one of the parties in criminal and civil trials by presenting evidence and arguing in court to support their client. As advisors, lawyers counsel their clients about their legal rights and obligations and suggest particular courses of action in business and personal matters. Whether acting as an advocate or an advisor, all attorneys research the intent of laws and judicial decisions and apply the law to the specific circumstances faced by their clients.

The more detailed aspects of a lawyer's job depend upon his or her field of specialization and position. Although all lawyers are licensed to represent parties in court, some appear in court more frequently than others. Trial lawyers, who specialize in trial work, must be able to think quickly and speak with ease and authority. In addition, familiarity with courtroom rules and strategy is particularly important in trial work. Still, trial lawyers spend the majority of their time outside the courtroom, conducting research, interviewing clients and witnesses, and handling other details in preparation for a trial.

Lawyers may specialize in a number of areas, such as bankruptcy, probate, international, elder, or environmental law. Those specializing in environmental law, for example, may represent interest groups, waste disposal companies, or construction firms in their dealings with the U.S. Environmental Protection Agency and other Federal and State agencies. These lawyers help clients prepare and file for licenses and applications for approval before certain activities may occur. Some lawyers specialize in the growing field of intellectual property, helping to protect clients' claims to copyrights, artwork under contract, product designs, and computer programs. Other lawyers advise insurance companies about the legality of insurance transactions, guiding the company in writing insurance policies to conform to the law and to protect the companies from unwarranted claims. When claims are filed against insurance companies, these attorneys review the claims and represent the companies in court.

Most lawyers are in private practice, concentrating on criminal or civil law. In criminal law, lawyers represent individuals who have been charged with crimes and argue their cases in courts of law. Attorneys dealing with civil law assist clients with litigation, wills, trusts, contracts, mortgages, titles, and leases. Other lawyers handle only public-interest cases—civil or criminal—concentrating on particular causes and choosing cases that might have an impact on the way law is applied. Lawyers are sometimes employed full time by a single client. If the client is a corporation, the lawyer is known as "house counsel" and usually advises the company concerning legal issues related to its business activities. These issues might involve patents, government regulations, contracts with other companies, property interests, or collective bargaining agreements with unions.

A significant number of attorneys are employed at the various levels of government. Some work for State attorneys general, prosecutors, and public defenders in criminal courts. At the Federal level, attorneys investigate cases for the U.S. Department of Justice and other agencies. Government lawyers also help develop programs, draft and interpret laws and legislation, establish enforcement procedures, and argue civil and criminal cases on behalf of the government.

Other lawyers work for legal aid societies—private, nonprofit organizations established to serve disadvantaged people. These lawyers generally handle civil, rather than criminal, cases.

Lawyers increasingly use various forms of technology to perform more efficiently. Although all lawyers continue to use law libraries to prepare cases, most supplement conventional printed sources with computer sources, such as the Internet and legal databases. Software is used to search this legal literature automatically and to identify legal texts relevant to a specific case. In litigation involving many supporting documents, lawyers may use computers to organize and index material. Lawyers must be geographically mobile and able to reach their clients in a timely matter, so they might use electronic filing, web and videoconferencing, and voice-recognition technology to share information more effectively.

Work environment. Lawyers do most of their work in offices, law libraries, and courtrooms. They sometimes meet in clients' homes or places of business and, when necessary, in hospitals or prisons. They may travel to attend meetings, gather evidence, and appear before courts, legislative bodies, and other authorities. They may also face particularly heavy pressure when a case is being tried. Preparation for court includes understanding the latest laws and judicial decisions.

Salaried lawyers usually have structured work schedules. Lawyers who are in private practice may work irregular hours while conducting research, conferring with clients, or preparing briefs during nonoffice hours. Lawyers often work long hours; of those who work full time, about 37 percent work 50 hours or more per week.

Training, Other Qualifications, and Advancement

Formal requirements to become a lawyer usually include a 4-year college degree, 3 years of law school, and passing a written bar examination; however, some requirements may vary by State. Competition for admission to most law schools is intense. Federal courts and agencies set their own qualifications for those practicing before or in them.

Education and training. Becoming a lawyer usually takes 7 years of full-time study after high school—4 years of undergraduate study, followed by 3 years of law school. Law school applicants must have a bachelor's degree to qualify for admission. To meet the needs of students who can attend only part time, a number of law schools have night or part-time divisions.

Although there is no recommended "prelaw" undergraduate major, prospective lawyers should develop proficiency in writing and speaking, reading, researching, analyzing, and thinking logically—skills needed to succeed both in law school and in the law. Regardless of major, a multidisciplinary background is recommended. Courses in English, foreign languages, public speaking, government, philosophy, history, economics, mathematics, and computer science, among others, are useful. Students interested in a particular aspect of law may find related courses helpful. For example, prospective patent lawyers need a strong background in engineering or science, and future tax lawyers must have extensive knowledge of accounting.

Acceptance by most law schools depends on the applicant's ability to demonstrate an aptitude for the study of law, usually through undergraduate grades, the Law School Admission Test (LSAT), the quality of the applicant's undergraduate school, any prior work experience, and sometimes, a personal interview. However, law schools vary in the weight they place on each of these and other factors.

All law schools approved by the American Bar Association require applicants to take the LSAT. As of 2006, there were 195 ABA-accredited law schools; others were approved by State authorities only. Nearly all law schools require applicants to have certified transcripts sent to the Law School Data Assembly Service, which then submits the applicants' LSAT scores and their standardized records of college grades to the law schools of their choice. The Law School Admission Council administers both this service and the LSAT. Competition for admission to many law schools—especially the most prestigious ones—is usually intense, with the number of applicants greatly exceeding the number that can be admitted.

During the first year or year and a half of law school, students usually study core courses, such as constitutional law, contracts, property law, torts, civil procedure, and legal writing. In the remaining time, they may choose specialized courses in fields such as tax, labor, or corporate law. Law students often gain practical experience by participating in school-sponsored legal clinics; in the school's moot court competitions, in which students conduct appellate arguments; in practice trials under the supervision of experienced lawyers and judges; and through research and writing on legal issues for the school's law journals.

A number of law schools have clinical programs in which students gain legal experience through practice trials and projects under the supervision of lawyers and law school faculty. Law school clinical programs might include work in legal aid offices, for example, or on legislative committees. Part-time or summer clerkships in law firms, government agencies, and corporate legal departments also provide valuable experience. Such training can lead directly to a job after graduation and can help students decide what kind of practice best suits them. Law school graduates receive the degree of juris doctor (J.D.), a first professional degree.

Advanced law degrees may be desirable for those planning to specialize, research, or teach. Some law students pursue joint degree programs, which usually require an additional semester or year of study. Joint degree programs are offered in a number of areas, including business administration or public administration.

After graduation, lawyers must keep informed about legal and nonlegal developments that affect their practices. In 2006, 43 States and jurisdictions required lawyers to participate in mandatory continuing legal education. Many law schools and State and local bar associations provide continuing education courses that help lawyers stay abreast of recent developments. Some States allow continuing education credits to be obtained through participation in seminars on the Internet.

Licensure. To practice law in the courts of any State or other jurisdiction, a person must be licensed, or admitted to its bar, under rules established by the jurisdiction's highest court. All States require that applicants for admission to the bar pass a written bar examination; most States also require applicants to pass a separate written ethics examination. Lawyers who have been admitted to the bar in one State occasionally may be admitted to the bar in another without taking another examination if they meet the latter jurisdiction's standards of good moral character and a specified period of legal experience. In most cases, however, lawyers must pass the bar examination in each State in which they plan to practice. Federal courts and agencies set their own qualifications for those practicing before or in them.

To qualify for the bar examination in most States, an applicant must earn a college degree and graduate from a law school accredited by the American Bar Association (ABA) or the proper State authorities. ABA accreditation signifies that the law school, particularly its library and faculty, meets certain standards. With certain exceptions, graduates of schools not approved by the ABA are restricted to taking the bar examination and practicing in the State or other jurisdiction in which the school is located; most of these schools are in California.

Although there is no nationwide bar examination, 48 States, the District of Columbia, Guam, the Northern Mariana Islands, Puerto Rico, and the Virgin

Islands require the 6-hour Multistate Bar Examination (MBE) as part of their overall bar examination; the MBE is not required in Louisiana or Washington. The MBE covers a broad range of issues, and sometimes a locally prepared State bar examination is given in addition to it. The 3-hour Multistate Essay Examination (MEE) is used as part of the bar examination in several States. States vary in their use of MBE and MEE scores.

Many States also require Multistate Performance Testing to test the practical skills of beginning lawyers. Requirements vary by State, although the test usually is taken at the same time as the bar exam and is a one-time requirement.

In 2007, law school graduates in 52 jurisdictions were required to pass the Multistate Professional Responsibility Examination (MPRE), which tests their knowledge of the ABA codes on professional responsibility and judicial conduct. In some States, the MPRE may be taken during law school, usually after completing a course on legal ethics.

Other qualifications. The practice of law involves a great deal of responsibility. Individuals planning careers in law should like to work with people and be able to win the respect and confidence of their clients, associates, and the public. Perseverance, creativity, and reasoning ability also are essential to lawyers, who often analyze complex cases and handle new and unique legal problems.

Advancement. Most beginning lawyers start in salaried positions. Newly hired attorneys usually start as associates and work with more experienced lawyers or judges. After several years, some lawyers are admitted to partnership in their firm, which means they are partial owners of the firm, or go into practice for themselves. Some experienced lawyers are nominated or elected to judgeships. (See the section on judges, magistrates, and other judicial workers elsewhere in the Handbook.) Others become full-time law school faculty or administrators; a growing number of these lawyers have advanced degrees in other fields as well.

Some attorneys use their legal training in administrative or managerial positions in various departments of large corporations. A transfer from a corporation's legal department to another department often is viewed as a way to gain administrative experience and rise in the ranks of management.

EMPLOYMENT

Lawyers held about 761,000 jobs in 2006. Approximately 27 percent of lawyers were self-employed, practicing either as partners in law firms or in solo practices. Most salaried lawyers held positions in government, in law firms or other corporations, or in nonprofit organizations. Most government-employed lawyers worked at the local level. In the Federal Government, lawyers worked for many different agencies but were concentrated in the Departments of Justice, Treasury, and Defense. Many salaried lawyers working outside of government were employed as house counsel by public utilities, banks, insurance companies, real estate agencies, manufacturing firms, and other business firms and nonprofit organizations. Some also had part-time independent practices, while others worked part time as lawyers and full time in another occupation.

A relatively small number of trained attorneys work in law schools, and are not included in the employment estimate for lawyers. Most are faculty members who specialize in one or more subjects; however, some serve as administrators. Others work full time in nonacademic settings and teach part time. (For additional information, see the Handbook section on teachers—postsecondary.)

Job Outlook

Average employment growth is projected, but job competition is expected to be keen.

Employment change. Employment of lawyers is expected to grow 11 percent during the 2006-16 decade, about as fast as the average for all occupations. The growth in the population and in the level of business activity is expected create more legal transactions, civil disputes, and criminal cases. Job growth among lawyers also will result from increasing demand for legal services in such areas as health care, intellectual property, venture capital, energy, elder, antitrust, and environmental law. In addition, the wider availability and affordability of legal clinics should result in increased use of legal services by middle-income people. However, growth in demand for lawyers will be constrained as businesses increasingly use large accounting firms and paralegals to perform some of the same functions that lawyers do. For example, accounting firms may provide employee-benefit counseling, process documents, or handle various other services previously performed by a law firm. Also, mediation and dispute resolution increasingly are being used as alternatives to litigation.

Job growth for lawyers will continue to be concentrated in salaried jobs, as businesses and all levels of government employ a growing number of staff attorneys. Most salaried positions are in urban areas where government agencies, law firms, and big corporations are concentrated. The number of self-employed lawyers is expected to grow slowly, reflecting the difficulty of establishing a profitable new practice in the face of competition from larger, established law firms. Moreover, the growing complexity of law, which encourages specialization, along with the cost of maintaining up-to-date legal research materials, favors larger firms.

Job prospects. Competition for job openings should continue to be keen because of the large number of students graduating from law school each year. Graduates with superior academic records from highly regarded law schools will have the best job opportunities. Perhaps as a result of competition for attorney positions, lawyers are increasingly finding work in less traditional areas for which legal training is an asset, but not normally a requirement—for example, administrative, managerial, and business positions in banks, insurance firms, real estate companies, government agencies, and other organizations. Employment opportunities are expected to continue to arise in these organizations at a growing rate.

As in the past, some graduates may have to accept positions outside of their field of interest or for which they feel overqualified. Some recent law school graduates who have been unable to find permanent positions are turning to the growing number of temporary staffing firms that place attorneys in short-term jobs. This service allows companies to hire lawyers on an "as-needed" basis and permits beginning lawyers to develop practical skills.

Because of the keen competition for jobs, a law graduate's geographic mobility and work experience assume greater importance. The willingness to relocate may be an advantage in getting a job, but to be licensed in another State, a lawyer may have to take an additional State bar examination. In addition, employers increasingly seek graduates who have advanced law degrees and experience in a specialty, such as tax, patent, or admiralty law.

Job opportunities often are adversely affected by cyclical swings in the economy. During recessions, demand declines for some discretionary legal services, such as planning estates, drafting wills, and handling real estate transactions. Also, corporations are less likely to litigate cases when declining sales and profits restrict their budgets. Some corporations and law firms will not hire new attorneys until business improves, and these establishments may even cut staff to contain costs. Several factors, however, mitigate the overall impact of recessions on lawyers; during recessions, for example, individuals and corporations face other legal problems, such as bankruptcies, foreclosures, and divorces requiring legal action.

For lawyers who wish to work independently, establishing a new practice will probably be easiest in small towns and expanding suburban areas. In such communities, competition from larger, established law firms is likely to be less than in big cities, and new lawyers may find it easier to establish a reputation among potential clients.

EARNINGS

In May 2006, the median annual earnings of all wage-and-salaried lawyers were $102,470. The middle half of the occupation earned between $69,910 and $145,600. Median annual earnings in the industries employing the largest numbers of lawyers in May 2006 were:

Management of companies and enterprises	$128,610
Federal Government	119,240
Legal services	108,100
Local government	78,810
State government	75,840

Salaries of experienced attorneys vary widely according to the type, size, and location of their employer. Lawyers who own their own practices usually earn less than those who are partners in law firms. Lawyers starting their own practice may need to work part time in other occupations to supplement their income until their practice is well established.

Median salaries of lawyers 9 months after graduation from law school in 2005 varied by type of work, as follows:

All graduates	$60,000
Private practice	$85,000
Business	$60,000
Government	$46,158

Most salaried lawyers are provided health and life insurance, and contributions are made to retirement plans on their behalf. Lawyers who practice independently are covered only if they arrange and pay for such benefits themselves.

RELATED OCCUPATIONS

Legal training is necessary in many other occupations, including paralegals and legal assistants; law clerks; title examiners, abstractors, and searchers; and judges, magistrates, and other judicial workers.

SOURCES OF ADDITIONAL INFORMATION

Disclaimer:Links to non-BLS Internet sites are provided for your convenience and do not constitute an endorsement.

Information on law schools and a career in law may be obtained from the following organizations:

American Bar Association, 321 North Clark St., Chicago, IL 60610. Internet: http://www.abanet.org

National Association for Law Placement, 1025 Connecticut Ave. NW, Suite 1110, Washington, DC 20036. Internet: http://www.nalp.org

Information on the LSAT, the Law School Data Assembly Service, the law school application process, and financial aid available to law students may be obtained from:

Law School Admission Council, P.O. Box 40, Newtown, PA 18940. Internet: http://www.lsac.org

Information on obtaining positions as lawyers with the Federal Government is available from the Office of Personnel Management through USAJOBS, the Federal Government's official employment information system. This resource for locating and applying for job opportunities can be accessed through the Internet at http://www.usajobs.opm.gov or through an interactive voice response telephone system at (703) 724-1850 or TDD (978) 461-8404. These numbers are not toll free, and charges may result. For advice on how to find and apply for Federal jobs, see the Occupational Outlook Quarterly article "How to get a job in the Federal Government," online at http://www.bls.gov/opub/ooq/2004/summer/art01.pdf.

The requirements for admission to the bar in a particular State or other jurisdiction may be obtained at the State capital, from the clerk of the Supreme Court, or from the administrator of the State Board of Bar Examiners.

Source: Bureau of Labor Statistics, U.S. Department of Labor, Occupational Outlook Handbook, 2008-09 Edition, Lawyers, on the Internet at http://www.bls.gov/oco/ocos053.htm (visited November 09, 2008).

OPTOMETRISTS

Significant Points

- Admission to optometry school is competitive.
- To be licensed, optometrists must earn a Doctor of Optometry degree from an accredited optometry school and pass the appropriate exams administered by the National Board of Examiners in Optometry.
- Employment is expected to grow as fast as average in response to the vision care needs of a growing and aging population.

NATURE OF THE WORK

Optometrists, also known as doctors of optometry, or ODs, are the main providers of vision care. They examine people's eyes to diagnose vision problems, such as nearsightedness and farsightedness, and they test patients' depth and color perception and ability to focus and coordinate the eyes. Optometrists may prescribe eyeglasses or contact lenses, or they may prescribe or provide other treatments, such as vision therapy or low-vision rehabilitation.

Optometrists also test for glaucoma and other eye diseases and diagnose conditions caused by systemic diseases such as diabetes and high blood pressure, referring patients to other health practitioners as needed. They administer drugs to patients to aid in the diagnosis of vision problems and to treat eye diseases. Optometrists often provide preoperative and postoperative care to cataract patients, as well as to patients who have had laser vision correction or other eye surgery.

Most optometrists are in general practice. Some specialize in work with the elderly, children, or partially sighted persons who need specialized visual devices. Others develop and implement ways to protect workers' eyes from on-the-job strain or injury. Some specialize in contact lenses, sports vision, or vision therapy. A few teach optometry, perform research, or consult.

Most optometrists are private practitioners who also handle the business aspects of running an office, such as developing a patient base, hiring employees, keeping paper and electronic records, and ordering equipment and supplies. Optometrists who operate franchise optical stores also may have some of these duties.

Optometrists should not be confused with ophthalmologists or dispensing opticians. Ophthalmologists are physicians who perform eye surgery, as well as diagnose and treat eye diseases and injuries. Like optometrists, they also examine eyes and prescribe eyeglasses and contact lenses. Dispensing opticians fit and adjust eyeglasses and, in some States, may fit contact lenses according to prescriptions written by ophthalmologists or optometrists. (See the sections on physicians and surgeons; and opticians, dispensing, elsewhere in the Handbook.)

Work environment. Optometrists work in places—usually their own offices—that are clean, well lighted, and comfortable. Most full-time optometrists work about 40 hours a week. Many work weekends and evenings to suit the needs of patients. Emergency calls, once uncommon, have increased with the passage of therapeutic-drug laws expanding optometrists' ability to prescribe medications.

Optometrists who work in solo practice or with a partner tend to work longer hours because they must tend to administrative duties in addition to their medical ones. According to the American Optometric Association surveys, optometrists worked about 49 hours per week, on average, in 2004, and were available to see patients about 38 hours per week.

TRAINING, OTHER QUALIFICATIONS, AND ADVANCEMENT

The Doctor of Optometry degree requires the completion of a 4-year program at an accredited optometry school, preceded by at least 3 years of preoptometric study at an accredited college or university. All States require optometrists to be licensed.

Education and training. Optometrists need a Doctor of Optometry degree, which requires the completion of a 4-year program at an accredited optometry school. In 2006, there were 16 colleges of optometry in the U.S. and 1 in Puerto Rico that offered programs accredited by the Accreditation Council on Optometric Education of the American Optometric Association. Requirements for admission to optometry schools include college courses in English, mathematics, physics, chemistry, and biology. Because a strong background in science is important, many applicants to optometry school major in a science, such as biology or chemistry as undergraduates. Others major in another subject and take many science courses offering laboratory experience.

Admission to optometry school is competitive. Applicants must take the Optometry Admissions Test, which measures academic ability and scientific comprehension. As a result, most applicants take the test after their sophomore or junior year in college, allowing them an opportunity to take the test again and raise their score. A few applicants are accepted to optometry school after 3 years of college and complete their bachelor's degree while attending optometry school. However, most students accepted by a school or college of optometry have completed an undergraduate degree. Each institution has its own undergraduate prerequisites, so applicants should contact the school or college of their choice for specific requirements.

Optometry programs include classroom and laboratory study of health and visual sciences and clinical training in the diagnosis and treatment of eye disorders. Courses in pharmacology, optics, vision science, biochemistry, and systemic diseases are included.

One-year postgraduate clinical residency programs are available for optometrists who wish to obtain advanced clinical competence. Specialty areas for residency programs include family practice optometry, pediatric optometry, geriatric optometry, vision therapy and rehabilitation, low-vision rehabilitation, cornea and contact lenses, refractive and ocular surgery, primary eye care optometry, and ocular disease.

Licensure. All States and the District of Columbia require that optometrists be licensed. Applicants for a license must have a Doctor of Optometry degree from an accredited optometry school and must pass both a written National Board examination and a National, regional, or State clinical examination. The written and clinical examinations of the National Board of Examiners in Optometry usually are taken during the student's academic career. Many States also require applicants to pass an examination on relevant State laws. Licenses must be renewed every 1 to 3 years and, in all States, continuing education credits are needed for renewal.

Other qualifications. Business ability, self-discipline, and the ability to deal tactfully with patients are important for success. The work of optometrists also requires attention to detail and manual dexterity.

Advancement. Optometrists wishing to teach or conduct research may study for a master's degree or Ph.D. in visual science, physiological optics, neurophysiology, public health, health administration, health information and communication, or health education.

EMPLOYMENT

Optometrists held about 33,000 jobs in 2006. Salaried jobs for optometrists were primarily in offices of optometrists; offices of physicians, including ophthalmologists; and health and personal care stores, including optical goods stores. A few salaried jobs for optometrists were in hospitals, the Federal Government, or outpatient care centers including health maintenance organizations. Nearly 25 percent of optometrists are self-employed. According to a 2005 survey by the American Optometric Association most self-employed optometrists worked in private practice or in partnership with other health care professionals. A small number worked for optical chains or franchises or as independent contractors.

JOB OUTLOOK

Employment of optometrists is expected to grow as fast as average for all occupations through 2016, in response to the vision care needs of a growing and aging population. Greater recognition of the importance of vision care, along with growth in employee vision care plans, will also spur job growth.

Employment change. Employment of optometrists is projected to grow 11 percent between 2006 and 2016. A growing population that recognizes the importance of good eye care will increase demand for optometrists. Also, an increasing number of health insurance plans that include vision care, should generate more job growth.

As the population ages, there will likely be more visits to optometrists and ophthalmologists because of the onset of vision problems that occur at older ages, such as cataracts and glaucoma. In addition, increased incidences of diabetes and hypertension in the general population as well as in the elderly will generate greater demand for optometric services as these diseases often affect eyesight.

Employment of optometrists would grow more rapidly if not for productivity gains expected to allow each optometrist to see more patients. These expected gains stem from greater use of optometric assistants and other support personnel, who can reduce the amount of time optometrists need with each patient.

The increasing popularity of laser surgery to correct some vision problems may reduce some of the demand for optometrists as patients often do not require eyeglasses afterward. But optometrists still will be needed to provide preoperative and postoperative care for laser surgery patients.

Job prospects. Job opportunities for optometrists should be very good over the next decade. Demand is expected to be much higher, and because there are only 16 schools of optometry, the number of students who can get a degree in optometry is limited. In addition to growth, the need to replace optometrists who retire or leave the occupation for other reasons will create more employment opportunities.

EARNINGS

Median annual earnings of salaried optometrists were $91,040 in May 2006. The middle 50 percent earned between $66,530 and $118,490. Median annual earnings of salaried optometrists in offices of optometrists were $86,760.

Salaried optometrists tend to earn more initially than do optometrists who set up their own practices. In the long run, however, those in private practice usually earn more.

According to the American Optometric Association, median net annual income for all optometrists, including the self-employed, was $105,000 in 2006. The middle 50 percent earned between $84,000 and $150,000.

Self-employed optometrists, including those working in partnerships, must provide their own benefits. Optometrists employed by others typically enjoy paid vacation, sick leave, and pension contributions.

RELATED OCCUPATIONS

Other workers who apply scientific knowledge to prevent, diagnose, and treat disorders and injuries are chiropractors, dentists, physicians and surgeons, psychologists, podiatrists, and veterinarians.

SOURCES OF ADDITIONAL INFORMATION

Disclaimer:Links to non-BLS Internet sites are provided for your convenience and do not constitute an endorsement.

For information on optometry as a career and a list of accredited optometric institutions of education, contact:

Association of Schools and Colleges of Optometry, 6110 Executive Blvd., Suite 510, Rockville, MD 20852. Internet: http://www.opted.org

Additional career information is available from:

American Optometric Association, Educational Services, 243 North Lindbergh Blvd., St. Louis, MO 63141. Internet: http://www.aoa.org

The board of optometry in each State can supply information on licensing requirements.

For information on specific admission requirements and sources of financial aid, contact the admissions officers of individual optometry schools.

Source: Bureau of Labor Statistics, U.S. Department of Labor, Occupational Outlook Handbook, 2008-09 Edition, Optometrists, on the Internet at http://www.bls.gov/oco/ocos073.htm (visited November 09, 2008).

PHARMACISTS

Significant Points

- Excellent job opportunities are expected.
- Earnings are high, but some pharmacists are required to work nights, weekends, and holidays.
- Pharmacists are becoming more involved in counseling patients and planning drug therapy programs.

- A license is required; the prospective pharmacist must graduate from an accredited college of pharmacy and pass a series of examinations.

NATURE OF THE WORK

Pharmacists distribute prescription drugs to individuals. They also advise their patients, as well as physicians and other health practitioners, on the selection, dosages, interactions, and side effects of medications. Pharmacists monitor the health and progress of patients to ensure the safe and effective use of medication. Compounding—the actual mixing of ingredients to form medications—is a small part of a pharmacist's practice, because most medicines are produced by pharmaceutical companies in a standard dosage and drug delivery form. Most pharmacists work in a community setting, such as a retail drugstore, or in a health care facility, such as a hospital, nursing home, mental health institution, or neighborhood health clinic.

Pharmacists in community pharmacies dispense medications, counsel patients on the use of prescription and over-the-counter medications, and advise physicians about patients' medication therapy. They also advise patients about general health topics such as diet, exercise, and stress management, and provide information on products such as durable medical equipment or home health care supplies. In addition, they may complete third-party insurance forms and other paperwork. Those who own or manage community pharmacies may sell non-health-related merchandise, hire and supervise personnel, and oversee the general operation of the pharmacy. Some community pharmacists provide specialized services to help patients with conditions such as diabetes, asthma, smoking cessation, or high blood pressure; others also are trained to administer vaccinations.

Pharmacists in health care facilities dispense medications and advise the medical staff on the selection and effects of drugs. They may make sterile solutions to be administered intravenously. They also plan, monitor and evaluate drug programs or regimens. They may counsel hospitalized patients on the use of drugs before the patients are discharged.

Pharmacists who work in home health care monitor drug therapy and prepare infusions—solutions that are injected into patients—and other medications for use in the home.

Some pharmacists specialize in specific drug therapy areas, such as intravenous nutrition support, oncology (cancer), nuclear pharmacy (used for chemotherapy), geriatric pharmacy, and psychiatric pharmacy (the use of drugs to treat mental disorders).

Most pharmacists keep confidential computerized records of patients' drug therapies to prevent harmful drug interactions. Pharmacists are responsible for the accuracy of every prescription that is filled, but they often rely upon Pharmacy technicians and pharmacy aides to assist them in the dispensing process.

Thus, the pharmacist may delegate prescription-filling and administrative tasks and supervise their completion. Pharmacists also frequently oversee pharmacy students serving as interns.

Increasingly, pharmacists are pursuing nontraditional pharmacy work. Some are involved in research for pharmaceutical manufacturers, developing new drugs and testing their effects. Others work in marketing or sales, providing clients with expertise on the use, effectiveness, and possible side effects of drugs. Some pharmacists work for health insurance companies, developing pharmacy benefit packages and carrying out cost-benefit analyses on certain drugs. Other pharmacists work for the government, managed care organizations, public health care services, the armed services, or pharmacy associations. Finally, some pharmacists are employed full time or part time as college faculty, teaching classes and performing research in a wide range of areas.

Work environment. Pharmacists work in clean, well-lighted, and well-ventilated areas. Many pharmacists spend most of their workday on their feet. When working with sterile or dangerous pharmaceutical products, pharmacists wear gloves, masks, and other protective equipment.

Most full-time salaried pharmacists work approximately 40 hours a week, and about 10 percent work more than 50 hours. Many community and hospital pharmacies are open for extended hours or around the clock, so pharmacists may be required to work nights, weekends, and holidays. Consultant pharmacists may travel to nursing homes or other facilities to monitor patients' drug therapy. About 16 percent of pharmacists worked part time in 2006.

Training, Other Qualifications, and Advancement

A license is required in all States, the District of Columbia, and all U.S. territories. In order to obtain a license, pharmacists must earn a Doctor of Pharmacy (Pharm.D.) degree from a college of pharmacy and pass several examinations.

Education and training. Pharmacists must earn a Pharm.D. degree from an accredited college or school of pharmacy. The Pharm.D. degree has replaced the Bachelor of Pharmacy degree, which is no longer being awarded. To be admitted to a Pharm.D. program, an applicant must have completed at least 2 years of postsecondary study, although most applicants have completed 3 or more years. Other entry requirements usually include courses in mathematics and natural sciences, such as chemistry, biology, and physics, as well as courses in the humanities and social sciences. In 2007, 92 colleges and schools of pharmacy were accredited to confer degrees by the Accreditation Council for Pharmacy Education (ACPE). About 70 percent of Pharm.D. programs require applicants to take the Pharmacy College Admissions Test (PCAT).

Courses offered at colleges of pharmacy are designed to teach students about all aspects of drug therapy. In addition, students learn how to communicate with patients and other health care providers about drug information and patient care. Students also learn professional ethics, concepts of public health, and medication distribution systems management. In addition to receiving classroom instruction, students in Pharm.D. programs spend about one-forth of their time in a variety of pharmacy practice settings under the supervision of licensed pharmacists.

In the 2006–07 academic year, 70 colleges of pharmacy also awarded the master-of-science degree or the Ph.D. degree. Both degrees are awarded after the completion of a Pharm.D. degree and are designed for those who want additional clinical, laboratory, and research experience. Areas of graduate study include pharmaceutics and pharmaceutical chemistry (physical and chemical properties of drugs and dosage forms), pharmacology (effects of drugs on the body), and pharmacy administration. Many master's and Ph.D. degree holders go on to do research for a drug company or teach at a university.

Other options for pharmacy graduates who are interested in further training include 1-year or 2-year residency programs or fellowships. Pharmacy residencies are postgraduate training programs in pharmacy practice and usually require the completion of a research project. These programs are often mandatory for pharmacists who wish to work in hospitals. Pharmacy fellowships are highly individualized programs that are designed to prepare participants to work in a specialized area of pharmacy, such clinical practice or research laboratories. Some pharmacists who own their own pharmacy obtain a master's degree in business administration (MBA). Others may obtain a degree in public administration or public health.

Licensure. A license to practice pharmacy is required in all States, the District of Columbia, and all U.S. territories. To obtain a license, a prospective pharmacist must graduate from a college of pharmacy that is accredited by the ACPE and pass a series of examinations. All States, U.S. territories, and the District of Columbia require the North American Pharmacist Licensure Exam (NAPLEX), which tests pharmacy skills and knowledge. Forty-four States and the District of Columbia also require the Multistate Pharmacy Jurisprudence Exam (MPJE), which tests pharmacy law. Both exams are administered by the National Association of Boards of Pharmacy (NABP). Each of the eight States and territories that do not require the MJPE has its own pharmacy law exam. In addition to the NAPLEX and MPJE, some States and territories require additional exams that are unique to their jurisdiction.

All jurisdictions except California currently grant license transfers to qualified pharmacists who already are licensed by another jurisdiction. Many pharmacists are licensed to practice in more than one jurisdiction. Most jurisdictions require continuing education for license renewal. Persons interested in a career as a pharmacist should check with individual jurisdiction boards of pharmacy for details on license renewal requirements and license transfer procedures.

Graduates of foreign pharmacy schools may also qualify for licensure in some U.S. States and territories. These individuals must apply for certification from the Foreign Pharmacy Graduate Examination Committee (FPGEC). Once certified, they must pass the Foreign Pharmacy Graduate Equivalency Examination (FPGEE), Test of English as a Foreign Language (TOEFL) exam, and Test of Spoken English (TSE) exam. They then must pass all of the exams required by the licensing jurisdiction, such as the NAPLEX and MJPE. Applicants who graduated from programs accredited by the Canadian Council for Accreditation of Pharmacy Programs (CCAPP) between 1993 and 2004 are exempt from FPGEC certification and examination requirements.

Other qualifications. Prospective pharmacists should have scientific aptitude, good interpersonal skills, and a desire to help others. They also must be conscientious and pay close attention to detail, because the decisions they make affect human lives.

Advancement. In community pharmacies, pharmacists usually begin at the staff level. Pharmacists in chain drugstores may be promoted to pharmacy supervisor or manager at the store level, then to manager at the district or regional level, and later to an executive position within the chain's headquarters. Hospital pharmacists may advance to supervisory or administrative positions. After they gain experience and secure the necessary capital, some pharmacists become owners or part owners of independent pharmacies. Pharmacists in the pharmaceutical industry may advance in marketing, sales, research, quality control, production, or other areas.

EMPLOYMENT

Pharmacists held about 243,000 jobs in 2006. About 62 percent worked in community pharmacies that were either independently owned or part of a drugstore chain, grocery store, department store, or mass merchandiser. Most community pharmacists were salaried employees, but some were self-employed owners. About 23 percent of pharmacists worked in hospitals. A small proportion worked in mail-order and Internet pharmacies, pharmaceutical wholesalers, offices of physicians, and the Federal Government.

JOB OUTLOOK

Employment is expected to increase much faster than the average through 2016. As a result of rapid growth and the need to replace workers who leave the occupation, job prospects should be excellent.

Employment change. Employment of pharmacists is expected to grow by 22 percent between 2006 and 2016, which is much faster than the average for all occupations. The increasing numbers of middle-aged and elderly people—who use more prescription drugs than younger people—will continue to spur demand for pharmacists throughout the projection period. Other factors likely to increase the demand for pharmacists include scientific advances that will make more drug products available and the coverage of prescription drugs by a greater number of health insurance plans and Medicare.

As the use of prescription drugs increases, demand for pharmacists will grow in most practice settings, such as community pharmacies, hospital pharmacies, and mail-order pharmacies. As the population ages, assisted living facilities and home care organizations should see particularly rapid growth. Demand will also increase as cost conscious insurers, in an attempt to improve preventative care, use pharmacists in areas such as patient education and vaccination administration.

Demand is also increasing in managed care organizations where pharmacists analyze trends and patterns in medication use, and in pharmacoeconomics—the cost and benefit analysis of different drug therapies. New jobs also are being created in disease management—the development of new methods for curing and controlling diseases—and in sales and marketing. Rapid growth is also expected in pharmacy informatics—the use of information technology to improve patient care.

Job prospects. Excellent opportunities are expected for pharmacists over the 2006 to 2016 period. Job openings will result from rapid employment growth, and from the need to replace workers who retire or leave the occupation for other reasons.

EARNINGS

Median annual of wage-and-salary pharmacists in May 2006 were $94,520. The middle 50 percent earned between $83,180 and $108,140 a year. The lowest 10 percent earned less than $67,860, and the highest 10 percent earned more than $119,480 a year. Median annual earnings in the industries employing the largest numbers of pharmacists in May 2006 were:

Department stores	$99,050
Grocery stores	$95,600
Pharmacies and drug stores	$94,640
General medical and surgical hospitals	$93,640

According to a 2006 survey by Drug Topics Magazine, pharmacists in retail settings earned an average of $92,291 per year, while pharmacists in institutional settings earned an average of $97,545. Full-time pharmacists earned an average of $102,336, while part-time pharmacists earned an average of $55,589.

RELATED OCCUPATIONS

Pharmacy technicians and pharmacy aides also work in pharmacies. Persons in other professions who may work with pharmaceutical compounds include biological scientists, medical scientists, and chemists and materials scientists. Increasingly, pharmacists are involved in patient care and therapy, work that they have in common with physicians and surgeons.

SOURCES OF ADDITIONAL INFORMATION

Disclaimer:Links to non-BLS Internet sites are provided for your convenience and do not constitute an endorsement.

For information on pharmacy as a career, preprofessional and professional requirements, programs offered by colleges of pharmacy, and student financial aid, contact:

American Association of Colleges of Pharmacy, 1426 Prince St., Alexandria, VA 22314. Internet: http://www.aacp.org

General information on careers in pharmacy is available from:

American Society of Health-System Pharmacists, 7272 Wisconsin Ave., Bethesda, MD 20814. Internet: http://www.ashp.org

National Association of Chain Drug Stores, 413 N. Lee St., P.O. Box 1417-D49, Alexandria, VA 22313-1480. Internet: http://www.nacds.org

Academy of Managed Care Pharmacy, 100 North Pitt St., Suite 400, Alexandria, VA 22314. Internet: http://www.amcp.org

American Pharmacists Association, 1100 15th Street, N.W. Suite 400., Washington, DC 20005. Internet: http://www.aphanet.org

Information on the North American Pharmacist Licensure Exam (NAPLEX) and the Multistate Pharmacy Jurisprudence Exam (MPJE) is available from:

National Association of Boards of Pharmacy, 1600 Feehanville Dr., Mount Prospect, IL 60056. Internet: http://www.nabp.net

State licensure requirements are available from each State's board of pharmacy. Information on specific college entrance requirements, curriculums, and financial aid is available from any college of pharmacy.

Source: Bureau of Labor Statistics, U.S. Department of Labor, Occupational Outlook Handbook, 2008-09 Edition, Pharmacists, on the Internet at http://www.bls.gov/oco/ocos079.htm (visited November 09, 2008).

SALES ENGINEERS

Significant Points

- A bachelor's degree in engineering usually is required; many sales engineers have previous work experience in an engineering specialty.
- Projected employment growth will stem from the increasing numbers of technical products and services for sale.
- More job opportunities are expected in independent sales agencies.
- Earnings are typically based on a combination of salary and commission.

NATURE OF THE WORK

Many products and services, especially those purchased by large companies and institutions, are highly complex. Sales engineers—who also may be called manufacturers' agents, sales representatives, or technical sales support workers—work with the production, engineering, or research and development departments of their companies, or with independent sales firms, to determine how products and services could be designed or modified to suit customers' needs. They also may advise customers on how best to use the products or services provided.

Sales engineers sell and consult on technologically and scientifically advanced products. They should possess extensive knowledge of these products, including their components and processes. Sales engineers then use their technical skills to demonstrate to potential customers how and why the products or services they are selling would suit the customer better than competitors' products. Often, there may not be a directly competitive product. In these cases, the job of the sales engineer is to demonstrate to the customer the usefulness of the product or service—for example, how much money new production machinery would save.

Engineers apply the theories and principles of science and mathematics to technical problems. Their work is the link between scientific discoveries and commercial applications. Many sales engineers specialize in products that are related to their engineering specialty. For example, sales engineers selling chemical products may have chemical engineering backgrounds, while those selling business software or information systems may have degrees in computer engineering. (Information on engineers, including 17 engineering specialties, appears elsewhere in the Handbook.)

Many of the duties of sales engineers are similar to those of other salespersons. They must interest the client in purchasing their products, many of which are durable manufactured products such as turbines. Sales engineers often are teamed with other salespersons who concentrate on the marketing and sales, enabling the sales engineer to concentrate on the technical aspects of the job. By working on a sales team, each member is able to focus on his or her strengths and expertise. (Information on other sales occupations, including sales representatives, wholesale and manufacturing, appears elsewhere in the Handbook.)

Sales engineers tend to employ selling techniques that are different from those used by most other sales workers. They generally use a "consultative" style; that is, they focus on the client's problem and show how it could be solved or mitigated with their product or service. This selling style differs from the "benefits and features" method, whereby the salesperson describes the product and leaves the customer to decide how it would be useful.

In addition to maintaining current clients and attracting new ones, sales engineers help clients solve any problems that arise when the product is installed.

Afterward, they may continue to serve as a liaison between the client and their company. Increasingly, sales engineers are asked to undertake tasks related to sales, such as market research, because of their familiarity with clients' purchasing needs. Drawing on this same familiarity, sales engineers may help identify and develop new products.

Work environment. Sales engineers may work directly for manufacturers or service providers, or they may work in small independent sales firms. In an independent firm, they may sell complementary products from several different suppliers.

Workers in this occupation can encounter pressure and stress because their income and job security often depend directly on their success in sales and customer service. Many sales engineers work more than 40 hours per week to meet sales goals and client needs. Although the hours may be long and often irregular, many sales engineers have the freedom to determine their own schedules. Consequently, they often can arrange their appointments so that they can have time off when they want it.

Some sales engineers have large territories and travel extensively. Because sales regions may cover several States, sales engineers may be away from home for several days or even weeks at a time. Others work near their home base and travel mostly by car. International travel to secure contracts with foreign clients is becoming more common.

TRAINING, OTHER QUALIFICATIONS, AND ADVANCEMENT

Most sales engineers have a bachelor's degree in engineering, and many have previous work experience in an engineering specialty. New sales engineers may need some on-the-job training in sales or may work closely with a sales mentor familiar with company policies and practices before they can work on their own.

Education and training. A bachelor's degree in engineering usually is required to become a sales engineer. However, some workers with previous experience in sales combined with technical experience or training sometimes hold the title of sales engineer. Also, workers who have a degree in a science, such as chemistry, or even a degree in business with little or no previous sales experience, may be termed sales engineers.

Admissions requirements for undergraduate engineering schools include a solid background in mathematics (algebra, geometry, trigonometry, and calculus) and the physical sciences (biology, chemistry, and physics), as well as basic courses in English, social studies, humanities, and computer science. University programs vary in content, though all require the development of computer skills. Once a university has been selected, a student must choose an area of engineering in which to specialize. Some programs offer a general engineering curriculum; students then specialize on the job or in graduate school. Most engineering degrees are granted in electrical, mechanical, or civil engineering. However, engineers trained in one branch may work in related branches.

New graduates with engineering degrees may need sales experience and training before they can work independently as sales engineers. Training may involve teaming with a sales mentor who is familiar with the employer's business practices, customers, procedures, and company culture. After the training period has been completed, sales engineers may continue to partner with someone who lacks technical skills, yet excels in the art of sales.

It is important for sales engineers to continue their engineering and sales education throughout their careers. Much of their value to their employers depends on their knowledge of and ability to sell the latest technologies. Sales engineers in high-technology fields, such as information technology or advanced electronics, may find that technical knowledge rapidly becomes obsolete.

Other qualifications.. Many sales engineers first work as engineers. For some, engineering experience is necessary to obtain the technical background needed to sell their employers' products or services effectively. Others move into the occupation because it offers better earnings and advancement potential than engineering or because they are looking for a new challenge.

Advancement. Promotion may include a higher commission rate, larger sales territory, or elevation to the position of supervisor or marketing manager. Alternatively, sales engineers may leave their companies and form independent firms. Independent firms tend to be small, and relatively few sales engineers are self-employed.

Employment

Sales engineers held about 76,000 jobs in 2006. About 37 percent were employed in wholesale trade and another 26 percent were employed in the manufacturing industries. Smaller numbers of sales engineers worked in information industries, such as software publishing and telecommunications; professional, scientific, and technical services, such as computer systems design and related services; architectural, engineering, and related services; and other industries. Unlike workers in many other sales occupations, very few sales engineers are self-employed.

JOB OUTLOOK

Job growth for sales engineers is projected to be about average through 2016, and opportunities will be good in independent sales agencies because of the increase in outsourcing of sales departments by manufacturers.

Employment change. Employment of sales engineers is expected to grow by 9 percent between 2006 and 2016, which is about as fast as the average for all occupations. Projected employment growth stems from the increasing variety and technical nature of goods and services to be sold. Competitive pressures and advancing technology will force companies to improve and update product designs more frequently and to optimize their manufacturing and sales processes, and thus require the services of a sales engineer.

In wholesale trade, both outsourcing to independent sales agencies and the use of information technology are expected to create some job growth for sales engineers. Although outsourcing should lead to more jobs in independent agencies, employment growth for sales engineers in wholesale trade likely will be dampened by the increasing ability of businesses to find, order, and track shipments directly from wholesalers through the Internet, without assistance from sales engineers. However, since direct purchases from wholesalers are more likely to be non-scientific or non-technical products, their impact on sales engineers should remain somewhat limited.

Job prospects. Manufacturers, especially foreign manufacturers that sell their products in the United States, are expected to continue outsourcing more of their sales functions to independent sales agencies in an attempt to control costs. Additionally, since independent agencies can carry multiple lines of products, a single sales engineer can handle more products than the single product line they would have handled under a manufacturer. This should result in more job opportunities for sales engineers in independent agencies.

Employment opportunities may fluctuate from year to year because sales are affected by changing economic conditions, legislative issues, and consumer preferences. Prospects will be best for those with the appropriate knowledge or technical expertise, as well as the personal traits necessary for successful sales work. In addition to new positions created as companies expand their sales forces, some openings will arise each year from the need to replace sales engineers who transfer to other occupations or leave the labor force.

EARNINGS

Median annual earnings, including commissions, of wage and salary sales engineers were $77,720 in May 2006. The middle 50 percent earned between $59,490 and $100,280 a year. The lowest 10 percent earned less than $47,010, and the highest 10 percent earned more than $127,680 a year. Median annual earnings of those employed by firms in the computer systems design and related services industry were $90,950.

Compensation varies significantly by the type of firm and the product sold. Most employers offer a combination of salary and commission payments or a salary plus a bonus. Those working in independent sales companies may solely earn commissions. Commissions usually are based on the amount of sales, whereas bonuses may depend on individual performance, on the performance of all workers in the group or district, or on the company's performance. Earnings from commissions and bonuses may vary greatly from year to year, depending on sales ability, the demand for the company's products or services, and the overall economy.

In addition to their earnings, sales engineers who work for manufacturers usually are reimbursed for expenses such as transportation, meals, hotels, and customer entertainment. In addition to typical benefits, sales engineers may get personal use of a company car and frequent-flyer mileage. Some companies offer incentives such as free vacation trips or gifts for outstanding performance. Sales engineers who work in independent firms may have higher but less stable earnings and, often, relatively few benefits. Most independent sales engineers do not earn any income while on vacation.

RELATED OCCUPATIONS

Sales engineers must have sales ability and knowledge of the products and services they sell, as well as technical and analytical skills. Other occupations that require similar skills include advertising, marketing, promotions, public relations, and sales managers; engineers; insurance sales agents; purchasing managers, buyers and purchasing agents; real estate brokers and sales agents; sales representatives, wholesale and manufacturing; and securities, commodities, and financial services sales agents.

SOURCES OF ADDITIONAL INFORMATION

Disclaimer:Links to non-BLS Internet sites are provided for your convenience and do not constitute an endorsement.

Information on careers for manufacturers' representatives and agents is available from:

Manufacturers' Agents National Association, P.O. Box 3467, Laguna Hills, CA 92654. Internet: http://www.manaonline.org

Manufacturers' Representatives Educational Research Foundation, 8329 Cole St., Arvada, CO 80005. Internet: http://www.mrerf.org

Source: Bureau of Labor Statistics, U.S. Department of Labor, Occupational Outlook Handbook, 2008-09 Edition, Sales Engineers, on the Internet at http://www.bls.gov/oco/ocos123.htm (visited November 09, 2008).

BIBLIOGRAPHY

Aguilar, M. and Lorece Williams. "Factors Contributing to the Success and Achievement of Minority Women." *Affilia* 8 (1993): 410–423.

Alexander, Amy. *Fifty Black Women Who Changed America.* New Jersey: Birch Lane Press, 1999.

Association of American Medical Colleges. *Diversity in the Physician Workforce: Facts and Figures.* Washington, D.C.: Association of American Medical Colleges, 2006.

Awe, Susan. "Seven Secrets of Successful Women." *Literary Journal* 122 (1997):108.

Becker, Frances. *Twenty Black Women: A Profile of Contemporary Black Maryland Women.* Maryland: Gateway Press, 1978.

Bell, Ella and Stella Nkomo. *Our Separate Ways: Black and White Women and the Struggle for Professional Identity.* Massachusetts: Harvard Business School, 2001.

Brem, Marion. *Seven Greatest Truths About Successful Women.* New York: Penguin, 2001.

Brooks, Donna and L. Brooks. *Seven Secrets of Successful Women.* New York: McGraw Hill, 1997.

Caplan, Sonara. "Highly Successful Women Administrators." *National Association of Secondary School Principals Bulletin.* 83 (1998): 594–595.

Clarke, Caroline. *Take a Lesson: Today's Black Achievers on How They Made It and What They Learned Along the Way.* New York: John Wiley and Sons, 2000.

Cohen, Sarah. 1997. Seven Secrets of Successful Women." *Training and Development* 51 (1997): 59–60.

Commission on Racial and Ethnic Diversity in the Profession. *Miles to Go: Progress of Minorities in the Legal Profession.* Washington, D.C.: American Bar Association, 2005.

Cook, Sarah. 1998. "Cultivate the Habits of Highly Successful Women." *Women in Higher Education.* 7 (1998): 30.

Cook, Verna and Charlotte Brooks eds.. Distinguished Black Women. 3 vols. D.C.: Black Women in Sisterhood for Action Inc., 1991–1995, 1996.

Costello, Cynthia and Anne Stone eds.. *The American Women: 2001–2002.* Washington, D.C.: Women's Research and Education Institute, 2001.

Davis, Laura. Address to the American Association of Women in Community Colleges Region V conference, October 1998, quoted in Sarah Cook, 1998, 30.

De LaVergne, Suzanne. "Factors Affecting Upward Mobility of Minority Women in School Administration." Ph.D. dissertation, U.S. International University, 1991.

Elhart-Morrison, Dorothy. *No Mountain High Enough: Secrets of Successful African American Women.* California: Conari, 1997.

Elly, Janice and M. William. *What Every Successful Woman Knows: 12 Breakthrough Strategies to Get the Power and Ignite Your Career.* New York: McGraw Hill, 2001

Failde, Augusto and William Doyle. *Latino Success: Insights from 100 of America's Most Powerful Latino Business Professionals.* New York: Simon & Schuster, 1996.

Fairlie, Robert and Alicia Robb. *Race and Entrepreneurial Success: Black , Asian and White-Owned Businesses in the United States.* Cambridge: MIT Press, 2008.

Farr, Michael. *200 Best Jobs for College Graduates.* Indiana: JIST, 2006. With database work by Laurence Shatkin.

Featherman, Sandra. "Highly Successful Women Administrators-Inside Stories of How They Got There." *Women in Higher Education* 6(6) 1997: 23.

Field, John. *Social Capital.* London: Routledge, 2003.

Friedman, R. M. Kane, and D. B. Cornfield. "Social Support and Career Optimism: Examining the Effectiveness of Network Groups among Black Managers." *Human Relations* 51 (1998): 1155–1177.

Gallagher, Carol and Susan Galant. *Going to the Top. A Road Map for Success from America's Leading Women Executives.* New York: Viking, 2000.

General Accounting Office. *Human Capital: Diversity in the Federal SES and Senior Levels of the U.S. Postal Service.* Washington, D.C.: GAO, 2008.

Gilberd, Pamela. *The 11 Commandments of Wildly Successful Women.* New York: Macmillian, 1999.

———. *The Twelfth Commandments of Wildly Successful Women.* Masschusetts: Chandler House, 1996.

Goetz, David. "A Decent BET." *Broadcasting and Cable.* September 2007

Halcomb, Ruth. *Women Making It: Patterns and Profiles of Success.* New York: Atheneum, 1979.

Hall, Rashaun. "Talkin' BET with Debra Lee." *Billboard.* October 2005.

Harper, Betty. "Women and Women's Colleges: Is an Intervening Variable in the Reported Relationship?" *Sex Roles* 33 (1995): 489–497.

Healey, Joseph. *Race, Ethnicity, Gender and Class.* California: Pine Forge Press, 1995.

Higginson, Margaret and Thomas Quick. *The Ambitious Woman's Guide to a Successful Career.* 1975.

Hine, Darlene and Kathleen Thompson, eds. *Facts on File: Encyclopedia of Black Women in America.* Business and Professions. New York: Facts on File Inc., 1997.

Horsburg, Susan et al. "Rags to Riches." *People.* August 2004.

Jasso, Lorenzo. "Variables Related to Minority Attainment of the Principalship." Ph.D. dissertation. Drake University, 1992.

Jones, Charisse. "Owning the Airwaves." *Essence.* October 2008.

Landrum, Gene. *Profiles of Female Genius: Thirteen Creative Women Who Changed the World.* New York: Prometheus, 1996.

———. *Profiles of Black Success.* New York: Prometheus, 1999.

Ledman, R. E., M. Miller and D. R. Brown. "Successful Women and Women's Colleges: Is Three an Intervening Variable in a Reported Relationship?" *Sex Roles* 33 (1995): 489–497.

Lerner, Gerda. *Why History Matters.* New York: Oxford, 1999.

Lubetkin, Abe. "Success is about Risk-Taking." *Daily News Herald.* February 26, 2007.

Maynard, John. "Firmly Anchored." *The Washington Post.* July 30, 2006.

Merritt, Patricia. *Sister Power: How Phenomenal Black Women Are Rising to the Top.* New York: John Wiley, 1996.

Mikaelian, A. *Women Who Mean Business: Success Stories of Women Over Forty.* New York: William Morrow and Company.

Mitchell, Nikki. *The New Color of Success: Twenty Young Black Millionaires Tell You How They're Making It.* California: Prima, 1999.

Morrison, Ann. *The New Leaders: Guidelines on Leadership Diversity in America.* San Francisco: Jossey-Bass, 1992.

Naff, Katherine. "The Glass Ceiling Revisited: Determinants of Federal Job Advancement." *Policy Studies Review* 13 (Autumn/Winter 1995): 249–72.

Norment, Lynn. "Cathy Hughes: Ms. Radio." *Ebony,* May 2000.

Northcutt, Cecelia. *Successful Career Women.* New York: Greenwood Publishing Group, 1991.

President's Interagency Council on Women. *America's Commitment to Women.* Washington, D.C.: Government Printing Office, 2000.

Randolph, Laura. "Superwomen: How They Manage to Almost Do It All." *Ebony,* 1998.

Reid, S. A. "Big Footsteps, Sharp Focus, Bold Message: Jane Smith Succeeds Dorothy I. Height as Leader of Black Women's Council." *Atlanta Journal,* February 5, 1998.

Revere, A. B. "Black Women Superintendents in the United States 1984–85." *Journal of Negro Education* 56 (1986): 510–520.

Rimm, Sylvia. *How Jane Won: 55 Successful Women Show How They Grew From Ordinary Girls to Extraordinary Women.* New York: Crown Business, 2001. With Sara Rimm Kaufman.

Roberson, Ponchitta. "Career Paths and Profiles of Women as Senior Administrators in Higher Education." Ph.D. dissertation, George Washington University, 1998.

Roberts, Bari-Ellen and Jack White. *Roberts vs Texaco: A True Story of Race and Corporate America.* New York: Avon, 1999.

Sawyer, Mary. *The Harassment of Black Elected Officials: Ten Years Later.* D.C.: Voter Education and Registration Action Inc., 1989.

Smith, Jessie ed., *Notable Black American Women.* Michigan: Gale Press, 1996.

———. *Powerful Black Women.* Detroit: Visible Ink Press, 1996.

Texeira, Colleen. "Working in Politics." *Occupational Quarterly* 52 (2008): 1–14.

Tillman, Beverly and Leslie Cochran. "Desegregating Urban School Administration: A Pursuit of Equity for Black Women Superintendents." *Education and Urban Society* 33 (2000): 44–59.

Umstead, R. Thomas. "BET's Revival Mission: Debra Lee Tries to Shake Off the Networks Bad Rap." *Multichannel News,* October 2007.

U.S. Department of Commerce. *Some Evidence from Census 2000 about Earnings by Detailed Occupation for Men and Women. Census 2000 Special Report.* Washington, D.C.: U.S. Department of Commerce, Economic and Statistics Administration, 2004.

U.S. Department of Labor. Bureau of Labor Statistics. *Occupational Outlook Handbook 2008–2009.* Indiana: JIST, 2008.

U.S. General Accounting Office. Testimony Before the Subcommittee on Federal Work-
    force, Postal Service and the District of Columbia, Committee on Oversight and
    Government Reform, House of Representatives. *Human Capital: Diversity in the
    U.S. Federal SES and the Senior Levels of the U.S. Postal Service* by George Stalcup.
    GAO-07838T. Washington, D.C.: General Accounting Office, 2007.
Wolf-Wendel, Lia. "Models of Excellence." *The Journal of Higher Education* 69 (2000):
    141–186.
Wylie, Ellie. *Conversations with Uncommon Women.*. New York: American Management
    Association, 1999.

INDEX

ABOUT THE AUTHOR

Valencia Campbell is President of Decision Research, a consulting and research business. She has completed projects for the Baltimore Public School System, the National Science Foundation, the National Congress of Black Women, and the National Council of Negro Women. She has taught sociology courses at Howard University and Bowie State University. Her many awards include Governor's Citation for Work on the Improvement of the Status of Women, Woman of the Year for Southern Prince George's Business and Professional Women, WHUR Hometown Hero Award, 9to5 National Association of Working Women Awards, and a Presidential Appointment to the United Service Organization World Board of Governors from 2006–2008. She holds a Ph.D. and M.A. degree from Howard University and a B.A. degree from Virginia State University.